The Magical History of the Horse

The Magical History of the Horse

JANET FARRAR
and
VIRGINIA RUSSELL

ROBERT HALE · LONDON

First published in Great Britain 1992

ISBN 0–7090–4366–X

Robert Hale Limited
Clerkenwell House
Clerkenwell Green
London EC1R 0HT

Photoset in North Wales by
Derek Doyle & Associates, Mold, Clwyd.
Printed in Great Britain by
St Edmundsbury Press, Bury St Edmunds, Suffolk.
Bound by Hunter and Foulis.

Contents

In loving memory of
Frances Jane Russell
1913–1990

Illustrations

PICTURE CREDITS

Stewart Farrar: 1, 3, 5; Janet and Colin Bord: 2; Fortean Picture Library: 4, 6.

Introduction

Mankind has achieved fruitful and widespread symbiosis with three other mammal species – the dog, the cat, and the horse.

Centuries of living, working, and playing with these three species has affected their own evolution, so that their present characteristics differ a good deal from those of their wild cousins. A Derby winner, a Dalmatian dog, and a Persian cat bear only a distant resemblance to a steppe pony, a timber wolf, or a Scottish wildcat.

Of the three species, mankind has perhaps developed the widest spectrum of collaboration with the horse. Over the centuries, the horse has been extensively used in warfare, hunting, agriculture, transport, and sport. It has also been used as an outstanding symbol of class status – though that aspect has fortunately almost vanished.

In some of these aspects, the dog and the cat have been used marginally or not at all. That does not diminish their importance to us, or the affection in which we hold them, but the horse does seem to have a special position, if only because of the wide range of its usefulness to mankind.

It has always been human nature to interpret history, relationships, and psychology in terms of mythology and folklore. These are not ignorant superstitions as very often they express and encapsulate truths more vividly than does bare factual description. Cold analysis and categorization has its limitations. Without mythology, folklore, art, poetry and drama, our awareness of the world, and our interaction with it, would be grossly inadequate.

Humankind's interaction with the horse over the centuries has also borne fruit in much legend and folklore, and also in religious symbology. Many religions use animal symbols to express particular aspects of their faith – as Christianity does, for example, with the lamb and the dove. Such symbolism is found in everything from profound religions to simple fairytales.

In this book, we have attempted to explore the role the horse has played in such contexts. We hope you will find these human stories and customs at least entertaining; but we hope, too, that they may deepen your understanding of the relationship between humans and their agelong friend and partner, the horse.

Deepened understanding is what mythology, folklore and religion are all about.

Janet Farrar
Virginia Russell

Kells, Co. Meath, 1991.

I *The Horse Comes West*

Before the domestication of the horse and the camel, almost the only practicable means of long-distance movement was by water, whether slow-moving river or coastal sea. This fact accounts for the early importance of Egypt as a comparatively large-scale coherent civilization; the Nile, from the First Cataract downwards, is slow-moving and easily navigable, between highly fertile banks, protected on each side by arid desert, and leading at the Delta to the known world's most navigable sea – the Mediterranean.

With the domestication of transport animals, the situation was transformed. As Arnold Toynbee puts it (*Mankind and Mother Earth*, p.34), 'the three largest areas of steppe – the Eurasian, the Arabian, and the North-African – became almost as conductive as the sea itself ... With the aid of riding-animals, pack-carrying animals, and draft-animals, human beings could cross the steppe almost as rapidly as they could cross the sea.'

The first pictures and carvings of horses are found in European caves, and date from about 13,000 BC, but the horse eventually disappeared from Europe, and became virtually confined to Asia.

Horses for many millennia were only hunted for food. They seem to have been first domesticated by nomads on the steppes of Central Asia about 4000–3000 BC. The horse had already become extinct in America some 2000 years before this, which helps to explain why, when the arriving Europeans first discovered native Americans, they lived mainly in small communities – a social structure which use of the horse tends to break down. It also explains why Cortez overran Mexico so easily; the natives were terrified by the speed and power of his warhorses.

The Mexicans' first encounter with the horse was at the battle of Tabasco in 1619. Cortez and his small band confronted a greatly superior force of natives, but when the Mexicans saw the cavalry, they imagined horse and rider were a single creature, and turned and fled from such terrifying monsters. Cortez did well out of this in another way; the Mexicans came back next day, peacefully bringing gifts. (Among these were twenty women, including a beautiful and highly intelligent young one called Malinche. She and Cortez were immediately attracted to each other. He renamed her Marina, and she learned Castilian rapidly, becoming his loyal interpreter, secretary, and mistress.)

By about 1800 BC, the Eurasian nomads had gradually bred, from their first puny domesticated horses, beasts capable of carrying effective loads or armed men, and of drawing chariots with teams no larger than two. It was at this stage that they began pressing westwards on a serious scale. Pastoral nomadism was non-agricultural, so settled agriculture was an easy prey to its superior mobility and the military advantage of the chariot. Linguistic evidence suggests that many of the large-scale movements of the time – the incursions by the Hurrians of Eastern Turkey into Mesopotamia and Syria, the Kassite invasion of Mesopotamia, and the Hyksos overrunning of Egypt, for example – were the results of even greater pressure from behind.

Much evidence suggests that because the Balkan mountains, which overshadow northern Greece, would have made horse movement very difficult, the main route of these invasions was along the southern shores of the Black Sea and through what is today Asiatic Turkey. In fact, no traces of such invasion have been found along the Balkan route, while the excavation of Troy VI, for example, has produced both horse bones and Minyan ware (pottery unique to the immigrant nomads).

Some scholars believe that Troy VI, which was destroyed by a devastating earthquake in about 1300 BC, was the one which fell in the Trojan War commemorated by Homer. If so, it would at least mean that the famous Trojan Horse was not an anachronism. Or was the story of that Horse, which brought about the city's fall, in fact a memory of the part horses played in the overrunning of the whole area?

It is worth noting that in Homer's *Iliad*, the chariot was still only a means for carrying his heroes to the battlefield, and away from it at speed if the battle went against them. Its use in the battle itself apparently developed later.

Overall, once the large-scale movements had settled down, primitive Mediterranean society was transformed into more widely based civilizations by this horse-riding immigration of entire peoples from Central and Eastern Asia. Perhaps the only exception to this transformation was Egypt; for there, the unifying factor of the long, narrow, and fertile Nile valley had produced a large-scale unified culture earlier than elsewhere, so the impact of the horse was less, in spite of the temporary Hyksos conquest.

It was these invaders who also brought with them the Indo-European language out of which Greek as we know it developed.

The wall-paintings in the family tombs at Mycenae (one of the earliest large fortified towns in Europe) have many portrayals of horses, including the first pictures of two-wheeled war chariots ever to be found in Greece. These tombs date from about the sixteenth century BC.

In the ancient Persian Empire (c. 600–300 BC) the horse was held in very high esteem. Young men were taught from their fifth to their twentieth year, the three main essentials – horsemanship, archery, and telling the truth (apparently in that order of importance). Provincial tribute to the Empire was often paid in horses – Cappadocia, for example, supplying 1,500 a year. Persia was the first to use horses on a large scale as the basis of their postal system; they maintained many thousands of postal horses, and their system was later copied by the Romans, the Mongols, and others.

As the horse became an established element in Mediterranean culture, economically and politically, it also began to take over some of the symbolic roles earlier held by indigenous creatures. This progressive takeover was a worldwide phenomenon, reflecting the development of various cultures from hunting through primitive agriculture to herd-raising and so on. As Joseph Campbell puts it (*The Masks of God: A Primitive Mythology*, p.197):

> One of the most important as well as illuminating aspects of the prehistoric perspective opened by a comparative study of myth rests in the problem of the pig's taking on the role of the serpent as the sacred animal of the labyrinth – and after the pig the bull, and after the bull the horse.

One incidental phenomenon which the horse also brought to the West was trousers. They had been unknown in the Mediterranean world where men wore long or short togas or tunics. So the breeches of the invading Asiatics – much more convenient for agile horseback-riding – added to their alien and awesome appearance. Tight trousers became adopted by the Romans for cavalry wear; they were the normal uniform of the cream of Rome's cavalry, the Celtic auxiliaries.

Oddly enough, however, 'trousers seem to have been virtually unknown among the Irish aristocracy, although they were worn by the servants' (Anne Ross, *Everyday Life of the Pagan Celts*, p.58). The legendary Queen Medhbh of Connacht, and the historical Queen Boudicca of the Iceni, for example, were each described as wearing richly decorated, long, heavy cloaks, though both of them had strong equine associations.

It has to be added that the culture-transforming movement of the horse was not only westwards, but eastwards as well, though its greatest impact there came later.

Up to the second century BC, the Chinese had been long

accustomed to small horses related to the Przewalski breed of the steppes which were rarely bigger than thirteen hands. China's oldest written characters, on tortoise-shell and bones in the tombs of the Shang emperors of around 2000 BC, reveal that small horses were then already used to pull carts.

During the Ch'in and Western Han dynasties (221 BC to 8 AD), however, which united China and completed the Great Wall, Chinese armies pushed as far west as Sogdiana, between the rivers Oxus and Jaxartes. In 128 BC Chang Chi'ien, an emissary of the Emperor Wu Ti, was in Sogdiana and Ferghana. He reported to his Emperor on the fine horses that had been developed there.

It was not until the Emperor's forces had defeated the prince of the Ta-Yuan in Ferghana in 101 BC, however, that the Chinese were able to bring back some of these western horses, which were greatly superior to their native breed. Over the following century they were able to establish them with great success.

They became known as 'celestial' and 'blood-sweating' horses, and were the status symbol of wealthy and official families. Figurines of them, quite different in their artistic portrayal from earlier examples, were plentiful in the tombs of such people.

The decorations of such tombs often included portrayals of the official concerned moving around the territory for which he was responsible, in a magnificent horse-drawn carriage, escorted by large numbers of well-mounted horsemen and by the slightly less splendid carriages of his subordinates. The size of this escort was a measure of the dead man's importance.

Horses bred today in the north Caucasus seem to descend from the ancient Ferghana stock; they have the same narrow chests, sinewy build, and long legs as the 'celestial' horses of the Chinese tombs.

Domestication has almost completely eliminated the genuinely wild horse, as compared with the semi-wild but humanly supervised breeds such as the Dartmoor pony. The only survivors of the wild horse were discovered in 1897 by the Polish explorer Przewalski, on the Mongolian steppes. Known as Przewalski's horses or Equus przewalskii, few of them still roam wild, but they thrive and breed in captivity, and they are in no danger of extinction. Interestingly, they are very similar to the horses portrayed in the European cave paintings of 20,000 years ago.

II *The Horse in Pagan Times*

Among ancient peoples, including those to whom horses came late, owning and riding them was in general the privilege of the king, the chief, and the warrior aristocracy. In the military sphere (which enshrines ancient patterns more stubbornly than most) this still survives in the mounting of infantry officers on ceremonial occasions, even if only of the commander and his or her immediate entourage, as at the British parade of Trooping the Colour. Significantly, there seems to have been a widespread instinctive feeling that something was 'not quite right' when Queen Elizabeth appeared at the 1987 Trooping the Colour parade unmounted; the magic of the event had been impaired.

Inevitably, the horse's elevated social status made it (as we shall see in Chapter IV) the totem animal of many deities. In particular, of that widespread archetype the Goddess of Sovereignty, to whom the king must be ritually mated to confirm his kingship.

What the king was doing in this 'sacred marriage', in fact, was mating with Mother Earth in her local aspect – whether it was Isis (whose Egyptian name, Aset, means 'throne'), Ishtar, or the legendary Medhbh (Maeve) of Connacht (of whom it was said 'until Medhbh slept with the lad, Cormac was not king of Ireland').

This ritual royal mating in pagan times, by actual intercourse, was usually with a priestess representing the goddess (which the original of Medhbh would doubtless have been). This ritual is generally referred to by its Greek name of *hieros gamos* or 'sacred marriage'. A thinly disguised version of it is the story recorded in the biblical Book of Esther (which name, adopted on her royal marriage, is itself merely a version of Ishtar, the Assyro-Babylonian chief goddess).

There is at least one recorded instance of the mare, however, as the Goddess of Sovereignty's totem animal, fulfilling the function.

Giraldus Cambrensis, visiting Ireland in the thirteenth century, reported the mating of a new king with a mare, in Kenelcunnil in northern Ulster. He wrote, distastefully:

> Once all the people had been gathered together, a white mare was led into the middle of the crowd. Then, in full view of everybody, this person of highest rank approached the mare bestially, not like a prince but like a wild beast, not like a king but like an outlaw, and behaved just like an animal, without shame or prudence.
>
> Immediately afterwards, the mare was killed, carved up into pieces and thrown in boiling water. A bath was prepared for the king with the broth, and he sat in it while scraps of the meat were brought for him to eat and to share with the people around him. He was also washed with the broth and drank it, not with a cup or his hands, but directly with his mouth. Once this ritual had been performed, his rule and sovereignty were assured.

As Christianity gained control in Ireland, the more explicitly sexual expressions of the mating of the king with the Goddess of Sovereignty were trimmed away in about the sixth century; but the concept itself remained ineradicable from Irish mythology as long as Irish kingship survived (Kim McCone, *Pagan Past and Christian Present*, p.138).

A parallel practice, but with a sexual changeover, used to take place in India. The ritual, *asvamedha*, involved the sacrifice of a stallion, who was then stuffed with fabrics. All the king's wives circled round the corpse for a while, and then the first wife lay down beside it and both were covered over. She then put the horse's phallus into her own sexual parts. The roles are reversed from the Celtic practice, but the symbolic meaning is the same –

the horse (whether mare or stallion) bringing divine blessing on royalty.

Not all identifications of the horse with the right to kingship were as dramatic as these two rituals. A more subtle example was the Greek king Oenomanus, who would only give his daughter Hippodameia in marriage to the man who could beat him in a chariot race. Hippodameia sabotaged her father's chariot so that Pelops could beat him – Oenomanus being killed in the race. A typical myth concerning the Goddess-Queen who helps the aspiring Young King to overthrow his predecessor, the old king. Like many other fathers in mythology, Oenomanus has been told by an oracle that his son-in-law would slay him. So he used his winged horses (symbols of his authority, given to him by his divine father, the war god Ares) to fend off the threat. In this story, however, Hippodameia represents (on the old matrilinear principle) the heiress – the Goddess of Sovereignty, and her name means 'horse-tamer'. Oenomanus relies on the fact that the totem animals were given to him by the God of Violence, but in the end it is Hippodameia who controls them, and uses them to bestow the kingship on the hero of her own choice.

'The whole of this hippogamous idea', T.C. Lethbridge writes (*Witches: Investigating an Ancient Religion*, p.93) 'must be of immense age, dating perhaps from a time when the horse had been domesticated only recently.' (He coins the word 'hippogamous' to mean 'through mating with a horse'.) He concludes (ibid. pp.139–40) that 'in the Indian case the stallion represented the sun and the ritual was intended to endow the realm with fertility', whereas in the Irish case 'the anthropomorphic god had to be mated to the totem beast, who was the mother of the tribe' – and that the Irish ritual was the older one 'and belonged at one time to the matriarchal phase of society'.

(There is a distinction between 'matriarchal' and 'matrilinear', incidentally. Ancient Egypt, for example, had become patriarchal in historical times as the Pharaoh actually ruled but it was still matrilinear because the Queen was the heiress. That is why so many Pharaohs married their sisters, or even daughters – to validate their title – and why Julius Caesar and later Mark Antony married Cleopatra, to justify their rule in Egyptian eyes).

Strangely enough, the Egyptians – who used animals and birds as symbols of archetypal concepts more richly and colourfully than any other civilization – made very little use of the horse in this way. The horse appears in their art from the very beginning, particularly in drawings of the Pharaoh's chariot engaged in war or hunting; but no god or goddess is portrayed in equine form, though they assume every other animal guise from the cat and the serpent to the hawk and the bull. A possible explanation for this is Egypt's unique geographical nature – a long narrow Nile-valley strip of intense fertility, only a mile or two wide in places, and flanked on each side by sterile desert. In such an environment, the horse's prime asset – mobility – would have been of minor significance, and pasturage for its breeding on any substantial scale would have been hard to spare. The nearest approach to an equine deity was Set, who appeared as an ass. Significantly, Set represented the desert and destructiveness, and was the constant enemy of the deities of wisdom, fertility and resurrection, Osiris and Isis.

Back to ancient Greece for a story linking the horse with kingship in an unusual way. Candaules, king of Lydia, showed his young wife Nyssia naked to Gyges. The outraged queen told Gyges he must kill the king and take his place. According to Plato, Gyges descended into a chasm of the earth, where he found a brazen horse. Inside it he found the carcass of a man, from whose finger he took a brazen ring. When he put the ring on his finger, he became invisible. This enabled him to enter Candaules' bedchamber and kill him. He then married Nyssia and ruled Lydia for thirty-eight years (716–678 BC), amassing such wealth that his name became proverbial.

A hint from English history of the identification of the horse with kingship: the leaders of the fifth-century Anglo-Saxon invasion are named in the Anglo-Saxon Chronicle as Hengist and Horsa. But *hengst*, means 'stallion' and *horsa* means 'mare', and many scholars believe they were not historical figures at all, but symbols of that leadership. The Chronicle was compiled over a period several centuries after the invasion, and its account of it can be shown, on archaeological evidence alone, to be wildly inaccurate, and in places pure fiction, or a transferring and rewriting of much earlier traditions. So it is not surprising if symbolism became transformed into 'history'.

The Venerable Bede (672–735), in his *Ecclesiastic History of the English Nation*, gave an interesting if unwitting clue when he wrote:

> The first two commanders are said to have been Hengist and Horsa ... They were the sons of Victgilsus, whose father was Vecta, son of Woden; from whose stock the royal race of many provinces deduce their original.

Apart from the fact that a Saxon would have been unlikely to name a son 'Mare', Bede makes these two the grandchildren of Woden (the God from whom the Nordic warrior kings certainly claimed authority, if not actual descent). Did he realize what he was implying about the true nature of Hengist and Horsa? At least he wrote 'said to have been', unlike his usual definite statements.

In the Turkish Empire, the identification of the horse with leadership was precisely graded. The three ranks of Pasha were distinguished by the number of horsetails displayed as the holder's banner, called his Tug. The highest grade, such as a Grand Vizier, was known as a Beglerbeg (Prince of Princes), and was entitled to display three horsetails. The second grade, governor of a province, displayed two. The lowest grade, known as a Sanjak or Bey, was entitled to a one-horsetail banner. The horsetail or tails were carried on a gilt lance in front of the Pasha concerned.

When the horse was introduced to the American Indians, some tribes at least seem to have incorporated its symbology into the rites of adulthood. A chronological record kept from 1750 to 1835 by Hehaka ('Elk'), of the Mahto band of the Teton Sioux, noted the first use of horsetails on the hunka-pipe during the blooding of a boy-brave.

American Indians' personal names always have meaning and the horse soon entered into this symbology, too. The Indian hero Crazy Horse is probably the best-known example. Another is explained by Lame Deer (*Lame Deer, Sioux Medicine Man*, p.117 – see Bibliography under John Fire):

> Take our famous chief Man-Afraid-of-His-Horse. It sounds funny in English. Man-Afraid once led warriors in battle against the enemy who fled before him. The medicine men wanted to honor him and so they bestowed this name on him, which really means: He is so brave, so feared, that his enemies run away when merely seeing his horse, even if he is not on it. That is a powerful name. He had to live up to it.

Horses were highly prized. Lame Deer (ibid. p.144) tells of a highly respected midwife who was paid a horse, or its value, for each delivery. 'That woman was busy all the time. She was a good witch.'

In Europe and Asia, there were, of course, exceptions to the rule that horses were the monopoly of leadership. For example, among its first domesticators were those steppe tribes whose livelihood, and means of conquest, was the large-scale breeding of horses. In their case, the horse would be the totem of the tribe as a whole. The Celts, too, were great horse-breeders; British and Gallic cavalry were among the Roman army's finest auxiliaries.

In Britain, the name of the Iceni – the Celtic tribe of the warrior queen Boudicca (Boadicea) – is doubtless a Latinization of Eachanaidh, which is Celtic for 'People of the Horse'. They would have been regarded with awe by their neighbours, and it may be significant that 'ickney' is still an East Anglian dialect word for 'proud or stuck-up'. When Boudicca's rebellion (which incidentally was provoked by the Romans' flouting of the matrilinear principle we mentioned above) was crushed by Suetonius' legions, some of the Iceni survivors fled to Scotland. There they became the MacEacherns, 'Sons of the Horse', in

Knapdale, Kintyre and the islands, where 'some of them still retain vague memories of being connected with horses in some supernatural way' (Lethbridge, op. cit., p.79).

The MacEacherns were not the only Scots whose name indicated horse-cult origins. In Roman times, there was a tribe in Kintyre called the Epidii – 'People of the Horse' – which is the same root as Epona, the 'Divine Mare'.

The Iceni were active horse-breeders, and horses feature on their coinage. Their horses were small, averaging about thirteen hands, and they were very successfully used in battle as chariot teams of a pair or sometimes four, but not as cavalry mounts.

There are some popular misconceptions about these chariots which are emphasized in Britain by the famous statue at the end of Westminster Bridge. They were not armed with scythes as scythed chariots were found only in Caledonia (and that only according to Tacitus), and were unknown in the rest of Britain. The chariot of Boudicca's army was light, skilfully manoeuvred over uneven ground, and used to carry an armed man at speed into the ranks of the enemy infantry, where he dismounted to fight. The effect on the heavily armed and slower-moving Romans was frightening, as Julius Caesar testifies.

It is interesting that Plato, in the account of the legendary Atlantis, allegedly from Egyptian archives, which he gives in his work *Kritias*, says that the Atlanteans had 'ten thousand battle chariots', including 'double-harness ones without a seat, which could carry a lightly armed warrior and next to him the driver of the two horses'. Such chariots did not appear in Celtic warfare until after Plato's time, and Ancient Greek war chariots were normally single-horsed, so the type he describes would have been foreign to him. Egyptian chariots, however, were as he describes from the beginning of the eighteenth dynasty (about 1580 BC). One may doubt the reality of Atlantis, but at least Plato's claim that his source of information was Egyptian appears to be genuine.

A legendary warrior queen with equine associations was Hippolyte, Queen of the Amazons, who was defeated by

Herakles. Her name means 'untethered mare'. The masculine equivalent of this name was borne by Hippolytus ('untethered stallion'), a young hero loved by the goddess Artemis. He was trampled to death by his own chariot team, and Artemis appealed to the physician Aesculepius to bring him back to life by his arts. Zeus was furious at the idea of a mortal escaping death, but Artemis hid Hippolytus, changed his appearance, and renamed him Virbius. In this disguise he became king of Nemi in Italy, where he dedicated a shrine to his divine patroness, and had a son also called Virbius who returned to the equestrian motif by driving a team of fiery steeds in the war against Troy. Virbius became worshipped as a god in Nemi and Campania.

Both these legends bear the stamp of having evolved from much older, pre-patriarchal myths. The Virbius pattern, for example, is that of the sacrificial death of the Old King, to be succeeded by the Young Hero, his own reborn self. Horses were barred from the Arician shrine, sacred to Virbius/Hippolytus, but Frazer (*The Golden Bough*, page 626) infers that this would be a taboo to heighten the one exception, an annual sacrifice there of a horse as symbol of the god himself. The Hippolytus story reappears in that of the Christian Saint Hippolytus.

The sacredness of the horse to the Celts, Saxons, and Danes alike, the principal ancestors of today's Britain, survives in the marked British (and Irish) reluctance to eat horseflesh, which resisted even the wartime efforts to ease rationing by trying to make it popular. There is no particular culinary reason for this prejudice, which is not shared by many of Britain's neighbours, but it seems embedded in our chromosomes.

It was not the Celtic habit to build permanent shrines of stone, except in those areas – Gaul in particular – which had become Romanized. In such places, where the occasional Romano-Celtic stone shrine is found (for example the temple at Roquepertuse in the Bouches du Rhone area in France, dating back to about the fourth century BC) horses' heads are among the bas-reliefs. Also found are small bronzes of horses with riders, possibly used as votive offerings. So the few surviving

Celtic religious structures emphasize yet again the ritual and symbolic importance of the horse.

It was a Celtic belief that the newly dead rode to the underworld on horseback.

Many wells were used to receive sacrificial offerings. For example, the figure of a horseman has been recovered from the bottom of a well at Tripontium (Cave's Head), Warwick, and horses' bones from several wells in Denmark.

Even domestic artefacts such as the twelve inch bronze-bound wooden bucket found at Alresford in Hampshire are frequently decorated with stylized horses' heads, and many Celtic coins figure horses.

This emphasis on the horse had existed at least as early as the La Tene period, about 500 BC, whose metalwork is rich in horse images. Often the horse is accompanied by a crane, both being solar symbols, and this may account for the fact that many Celtic stylized horse representations have rather beak-shaped heads – perhaps the two were being combined into one symbol, as are the horse and the man in the Centaur. (The Celts did not have Sun gods and goddesses as such; the Sun was used as a symbol of many deities' attributes, such as healing, wisdom and fertility. The only deities who were actually identified with material phenomena were the river goddesses. The river Boyne was the goddess Boann, material and spiritual natures of the same entity, so to speak, the Shannon was the goddess Sionan, and so on.)

The horse was particularly associated with war gods, but also, as we shall see in Chapter IV, with fertility goddesses and above all with Epona.

In Gaul, horses captured in war were often sacrificed to the appropriate war god, or to a river god, by drowning.

Red was the colour of death for the Celts, and in many stories red horses, ridden by red-haired men in red garments, appeared as omens of somebody approaching doom. (Compare the blood-red Horse of the Apocalypse – see p.71.)

A typical example comes from the Irish tale *Togal Bruidne*

Da Derga (The Destruction of Derga's Hostel), in which King Conaire encounters an omen in the shape of 'na tri Deirg' (the three Reds). They are three red-haired men, wearing red garments, and riding red horses. Conaire's son chases them but cannot overtake them, and they tell him: 'We ride the steeds of Donn Detscorach; though we are alive, we are dead.'

The urine of divine horses was said to be able to create wells and even lakes. The magic horse of the Irish god of love, Oengus mac Óg, urinated to form a well, and a woman was left in charge of it. When she forgot to secure the cover, the well burst forth and formed Lough Neagh. Another well, created by the urine of the horse of the god Midir, also overflowed and formed Lough Ri, named after a man called Ri ('King') who was drowned during its formation.

Early Welsh Triads have several references to magical horses, for example:

> Three bestowed horses of the island of Britain;
> Slender Grey, horse of Caswallawn son of Beli,
> Pale Yellow of the Stud, horse of Lleu Skilful-Hand,
> And Host Splitter, horse of Caradawg Strong-Arm.
>
> Three plundered horses of the island of Britain;
> Cloven-Hoof, horse of Owain son of Urien,
> Long-Tongue, horse of Cadwallawn son of Cadfan,
> And Bucheslom, horse of Gwgawn of the Red Sword.

Other Triads describe horses who carried a remarkable number of riders, such as Black Moro, horse of Elidir Mwynfawr. This horse took seven and a half people from Penllech in the North to Penllech in Monmouthshire – the half person being one who swam with two hands grasping the horse's cropper.

The horse was also sacred to the Goddess among the Picts of Scotland. Horses appear on many Pictish symbol stones, such as the Hilton of Cabdoll Stone on the Moray Firth in Ross and Cromarty, and the Aberlemno Churchyard Stone in north-east

Forfar. When ridden by men, they seem to refer to hunting or war; but many female riders clearly picture the Goddess – some, such as the Aberlemno example, being flanked by the Goddess symbols of the mirror and comb.

Incidentally the Picts represent a further example of an animal's prehistoric sacredness still having lingering effects today. Murry Hope (*Practical Celtic Magic*, p.49) tells us that among the Picts, the boar was another important animal 'sacred to the Cailleach, which is why many Scottish people eschew the eating of pork'. ('Cailleach' in both Scottish and Irish Gaelic means literally 'old woman', but is often used to mean 'witch' or 'Goddess' in the wisdom aspect of either.)

Sacred throughout these islands the horse certainly was – taboo for ordinary eating – but consecrated ritual fare at an annual horse feast. At such a feast, to consume the flesh of the totem animal would be a holy communion with the God or Goddess whose totem it was. (Ritual partaking of a symbolic representation of the flesh and blood of the God has, of course, been a feature of many religions, from Cretan to Christian.) This custom, too, survived stubbornly in places. In Denmark in the Middle Ages, for example, there was still a three-day horse feast, banned by the Church, but enthusiastically observed by the lower classes, and preceded by the ritual sprinkling of horse's blood to the south and east – 'which explains the horse as an incarnation of the Spirit of the Solar Year, son of the Mare-Goddess' (Robert Graves, *The White Goddess*, p.385).

To the nomadic, horse-dependent Indo-European peoples of Asia, and to many of the peoples they later conquered and whose cultures and mythology they influenced, the Sun was envisaged as a heavenly king eternally riding the skies in his horse-drawn war chariot. Thus the horse indeed represented 'the Spirit of the Solar Year'.

The horse is one of the Seven Treasures of Buddhism, representing the Fire element and the South station. This identification of the horse with the Fire element is echoed in St. Michael's patronage of horses and horsemen, for in the shadowy overlap between Christianity and paganism, Michael rules that element.

Yet the horse is identified with the Water element, too – especially among the Celts and the Greeks. Celtic water-horses are usually dangerous. The Isle of Man (named after the Celtic sea god Mannanán mac Lir) is haunted by the cabbyl ushtey or water-horse, often seen on land and looking just like an ordinary horse. If you mount him, however, he will carry you into a river or out to sea and you will never be seen again. The Scottish kelpie or water-sprite would often take the shape of a horse and offer travellers a ride; those who accepted would be dragged under water. At Buckland in Surrey, a red-stained rock near a stream is said once to have belonged to a water-horse called the Buckland Shag, who murdered people on top of it.

A malevolent spirit who works the other way round is the colt-pixie. It appears either in human form, or as a shaggy colt, and lures horses to their doom.

The Irish augh-ishka (in Gaelic each-uisce, 'water-horse') is less alarming. It comes out of the water to canter along the beach or through fields, and if you can catch one it makes a fine mount. You must keep it away from the sight of water, or it will return there with you on its back. In this it is not unlike the Irish mermaid – merrow, maighdean mhara, 'maid of the sea' – who wears a little red cap and sometimes marries a human and makes him a good wife. He must hide her cap, however, for if she gets it back she will return to the sea. (Water-horses in folklore are more fully dealt with in Chapter VIII)

The Greeks associated the horse with both Fire and Water. As the sun god Helios journeyed in a horse-drawn chariot, so did Poseidon, ruler of the sea. His team had golden manes and were shod with bronze. His wife Amphitrite was also drawn by horses. Poseidon had strong equine associations, as we shall see in Chapter IV.

For the Chinese, the horse is the symbol for perseverance and speed, and it was very much the totem of the invading Manchu dynasty, whose cavalry was the major factor in their takeover of

China. They introduced the familiar Chinese pigtail in imitation of the horsetail, and the Manchu sleeve is patterned on the shape of the horseshoe.

Unlike Western astrology, where the only significant appearance of the horse is in its fantasy form as a centaur in Sagittarius symbols, the horse plays an important role in Chinese astrology. The Chinese system is based on a repeated twelve-yearly cycle, each year being allocated to an animal – Rat, Buffalo, Tiger, Cat, Dragon, Snake, Horse, Goat, Monkey, Rooster, Dog and Pig, in that order.

The years are not exact calendar ones, since their beginnings and endings depend on Moon phases. Thus the Horse years of the twentieth century are a follows:

25 Jan 1906	–	12 Feb 1907
11 Feb 1918	–	31 Jan 1919
30 Jan 1930	–	16 Feb 1931
15 Feb 1942	–	4 Feb 1943
3 Feb 1954	–	23 Jan 1955
21 Jan 1966	–	8 Feb 1967
7 Feb 1978	–	27 Jan 1979
27 Jan 1990	–	14 Feb 1991

Of these, two are special – 1906 and 1966 – being known as Years of the Fire Horse. People born in a Year of the Fire Horse will have the same characteristics as other Horse people, but accentuated – the good as well as the bad points. The Horse is the only creature of the twelve to have such special years.

Horse people are said to be quick-witted, clever, and egotistical. They are determined workers and organizers, and efficient with money – but impatient, apt to lose interest suddenly and to switch over to some new target, partly because their confident image hides an inner insecurity. They tend to leave home young: the beginning and middle of their lives will be full of changing fortunes, but their later years relatively peaceful. They love being surrounded by people and, in particular, to be the focus of attention, and therefore often gravitate towards politics. Sexually attractive, they fall in love easily and obsessionally, becoming temporarily blinded to everything else, so they often get left stranded. If, however, they can balance their ambition for worldly success with that obsession, they may end up living happily.

They are advised that they can live amicably with Goat, Dog or Tiger people, but should avoid Rat people at all costs – particularly if they themselves are Fire Horse females.

For mankind as a whole – i.e. not merely for Horse year people – Horse years are times for consolidation, not for major changes, tradition maintains. One should develop plans already laid, not devise new ones. If you have new ideas in mind, you should not start working to achieve them until a more favourable year. (The year which follows the Horse, that of the Goat, is said to be advantageous for new discoveries and enterprises.) Horse years demand honesty and integrity, because breaches of these are apt to become public knowledge. Look after your health sensibly, and it should improve; neglect of it may cause trouble.

The relating of Chinese to western astrology suggests the following characteristics of Horse Year people born under the various Zodiacal signs.

Aries	– Fiery, even violent
Taurus	– Less egotistical than most, will make concessions
Gemini	– Restless, never finishing things
Cancer	– Over-sensitive
Leo	– Very capable, and self-centred
Virgo	– Efficient but unreliable
Libra	– Show-off
Scorpio	– Exciting and passionate
Sagittarius	– Plodding but unstable
Capricorn	– More responsible than most Horse people
Aquarius	– Fast-moving – watch it!
Pisces	– Unegotistical, will make concessions

One other Chinese system should be mentioned – the I Ching or Book of Changes – a divinatory and consultative method involving the sixty-four 'hexagrams' or possible combinations of six yang (male principle) and yin (female principle) lines. Hexagram two, The Receptive, consists entirely of yin lines, and is related symbolically to the mare. Its traditional judgement begins:

> The Receptive brings about sublime success,
> Furthering through the perseverance of a Mare.
> If the superior man undertakes something and tries to lead,
> He goes astray;
> But if he follows, he finds guidance.

The milk of any sacred or symbolically important animal is thought to have its own magic. Marco Polo, writing in his *Travels of the Holy Mares of Xanadu*, reported: 'The astrologers and idolaters have told the great Kublai Khan that he must make a libation of the milk of these mares every year on the 28th of August, flinging it into the air and on the earth, so that the spirits may have their share to drink. They must have this, it is said, in order that they may guard all his possessions, also the men and women, beasts, birds, crops, and everything besides.'

Any sacred animal is subject both to taboo and to sacrifice. Most notably, when a king or hero died, his horse used to be killed and burned or buried with him, as were his most precious possessions; all must enter the afterlife together. The Celts, as we have seen, believed that souls travelled on horseback to the Otherworld. Funereal sacrifice of a warlord's horse, so that he could be mounted in the afterlife, persisted in places well into the fourteenth century.

Some of the royal tombs of Mycenae in Greece which have been undisturbed by grave-robbers have given evidence of the kind of splendour in which a king was laid to rest. Weapons, food and wine would accompany him on his journey to the afterlife and, when all was prepared, the horses who had drawn the bier to the tomb would be slaughtered and their bodies carefully laid out facing one another.

A typical example of the practice among the Vikings is described in a late saga. Harold, a kinsman of King Ring, was killed in a great battle at Bravalla. His body was washed and placed in the chariot he had used in the fight. A large mound was raised and Harold's horse drew the chariot into it. The horse was then killed. The king left his own saddle by the body, telling Harold that he might ride or drive into Valhalla, whichever pleased him best. After a memorial feast, the nobles and warriors threw gold and silver rings, and good weapons, into the mound, which was then sealed up.

This attitude survives, though harmlessly from the horses' point of view, in military funerals today, in the custom of the dead man's horse carrying his master's boots, reversed on each side of the saddle.

The tradition has survived more directly than that, however, in the widespread reports of outstanding personalities being buried with, or mounted on, their favourite horse. Some of these tales are true, some apocryphal, but the apocryphal ones are just as interesting as evidence of the stubbornness of the tradition.

Two (factual) examples of this come from the authors' own experience. Virginia's mother was a Stewart of Mount Pleasant, New South Wales, and Virginia's great-grandfather, Major-General William Stewart, was Lieutenant-Governor of the colony. He was buried with his horse – and according to Virginia's grandfather, mounted upright on it.

Janet was a pupil of the Royal Wanstead School, which occupied Hyde Hall, Sawbridgeworth, Hertfordshire. A notorious squire of the Hall, Sir John Jocelyn, scandalously refused burial in the churchyard and was interred mounted on his favourite horse in the Hall woodlands, where his tombstone can still be seen. It was an initiation custom among the pupils to take new girls to the grave and tell them that on 18 December each year they would see Sir John's ghost riding down the drive. What they left the terrified newcomers to discover for themselves was that the school always broke up by 17 December!

To return to actual horse sacrifice, in particular the annual practice of it. In Rome, on 15 October each year, a chariot race was run on the Field of Mars, and the right-hand horse of the victorious team was stabbed with a spear as a sacrifice to Mars to ensure a good harvest. Its head was cut off and adorned with loaves, and two wards of the city contended for its possession. The blood was caught and kept till 21 April, when Vestal Virgins mixed it with the blood of foetal calves and gave it to shepherds to fumigate their flocks. (This apparently strange association of the God of War with fertility is explained by the fact that Mars was originally a god of sprouting vegetation, Mars Sylvanus 'Mars of the Woods'. March, the spring month, is named after him. He became a god of war by symbolizing the vigorous defence of the Romans' fertile lands, and this function in due course overshadowed his earlier one.)

The custom is paralleled as far away as Sumatra, where the Bataks would sacrifice a red horse or a buffalo to purify the land. A man would sometimes be bound beside the animal, and after its sacrifice he would be driven away as a scapegoat to rid the tribe of the year's sins.

In western Europe, as late as the eighteenth century, horses were burned alive as a sacrifice to ensure the health and safety of the rest of the horses and livestock.

Horses were sacrificed annually to the Hindu fire god Agni (from whose Sanskrit name, via Indo-European, the root of the word 'ignite' seems to stem).

Horse sacrifice among the nomadic tribes of the Altai Mountains in Central Asia persisted into the twentieth century. The Soviet authorities had to organize a propaganda campaign against it in the 1920s. In accordance with the official atheism of the time, they displayed posters of flayed horses on poles, with the caption: 'There are no gods. No sacrifices of horses will deliver you from your need.'

This custom was a remote survival of a practice of the

Scythians who used to inhabit large areas of what is now European and Asiatic Russia.

> The Scythians had methods of sacrificing horses which were remarkably unpleasing. They threaded the unfortunate beasts on long poles and raised them into the air ... According to Herodotus, many men and horses were sacrificed at the funeral of a Scythian king, stuffed and pegged up round his burial mound. The whole group was probably intended to accompany him as a present to their deity.
>
> (T.C. Lethbridge, *Witches: Investigating an Ancient Religion*, p.118.)

(It might be added here that the title of Lethbridge's work is a little unfortunate when it comes to items such as this. The book's scope is much wider than witchcraft, and so far as we can discover witches have never impaled horses on poles!)

In voodoo symbology, horse-riding is a metaphor for possession by a loa, or spiritual entity. The person possessed is referred to as the cheval or ch'wl (horse), and the loa is the rider who 'mounts' him or her. Voodoo thinking does not envisage possession by a loa merely in terms of trance or shamanism; the material world, including human bodies, is seen as inanimate and purposeless without such possession or infusion at all levels.

Voodoo is African with elements of Christian symbology integrated into it. The African deities which the slaves brought across the Atlantic were mainly Yoruba ones from Nigeria, including the supreme God Olorun, the heavenly Obatala and the Earth Mother Odudua, and their son Aganju and daughter Yemanja. Yemanja became the Universal Mother, more important even than Odudua, and one of the strongest survivors of the Atlantic crossing.

Horses appear in Yoruba mythology – for example, in the story of the curse which fell upon the kingdom of the thunder God Shango, one of Yoruba's many children, when his servants accused Obatala (who was disguised as a human) of stealing a horse he was feeding out of pity, and imprisoned him. The crops withered, the lakes dried, the women became sterile, and

Shango became impotent. When Shango recognized his grandfather and apologized, the curse was lifted. Shango was a great horseman, usually depicted mounted.

Another of Yoruba's offspring was Ogun, God of war, metal and blacksmiths. The Yorubas, having weapons of bronze, were able to conquer many other tribes. The traditional sacrifice to Ogun was a dog, and blacksmiths in Nigeria today often display a dog's skull in honour of their patron.

Renaissance art was much influenced by pagan themes, and one piece of symbolism which appeared in it was that of the bridled horse, signifying animal passions under control. A typical example is Veronese's painting of Mars and Venus which hangs in the Metropolitan Museum of Art, New York. It shows Mars, signifying strength, submissive to Venus who signifies love. To one side of them, Cupid holds the bridle of a horse which has no apparent relevance to the picture except to symbolize and emphasize its message.

III *Fantasy Forms*

Divine horses, in Classical and other mythologies, tend to be winged – an added emphasis to the admired equine qualities of speed, stamina, and resistance to taming. the outstanding individual example of the winged horse is the Greek Pegasus.

Pegasus was the offspring of the sea god Poseidon and Medusa the Gorgon – though not by the usual process of birth. Poseidon made love to Medusa (then still an attractive woman) in Athene's own temple. Athene, infuriated by this sacrilege, turned Medusa into a terrifying snake-headed monster whose glance turned men to stone. Later Athene helped the hero Perseus to kill her, and from the blood which gushed from her severed neck, the giant Chrysaor and the winged horse Pegasus were born. Athene marked her share in the victory by fixing Medusa's head on her shield.

Pegasus became associated with the Muses, and particularly with the inspiration of poets. On their mountain home of Helicon, the spring Hippocrene ('horse-fountain') sprang from his hoofprint; drinking from its waters fertilized poetic creativity. Hence Keats's longing:

> O for a beaker full of the warm South,
> Full of the true, the blushful Hippocrene,
> With beaded bubbles winking at the brim ...

Hippocrene's water also freshened the Muses' complexions when they washed in it.

This association of horses with magical or holy springs still persists.

Pegasus was not ridden till Bellerophon tamed him – again with the help of Athene, who gave him a magical golden bridle. Mounted on him, Bellerophon killed the Chimaera – an apparently indestructible monster who had the head of a lion, the body of a goat, and the tail of a dragon. Bellerophon even tried to scale Olympus on his winged mount, but Zeus flung him to earth and he was made lame. Pegasus survived the incident, was taken to Olympus, and was promoted to being a constellation. Both Pegasus and Bellerophon were closely associated with Corinth, and Corinthian coins kept Pegasus on the obverse and Athene's head on the reverse, merely updating the designs from time to time.

Pegasus would appear to have been at an earlier stage a mare-goddess, concerned with the kindly aspect of death. Robert Graves (*The White Goddess*, p.384) points out: 'Pegasus, in fact, was originally called Aganippe. Aganos is a Homeric adjective applied to the shafts of Artemis and Apollo, meaning "giving a merciful death"; so Aganippe would mean "the Mare who destroys mercifully".'

Medusa, too, may have changed over the centuries. That she mothered a horse may be explained by her story being much older than the known grim legend. Hints of this are the tradition that she once competed in a beauty contest with Athene; the fact that before she became a monster, Poseidon loved her; and evidence that the Gorgon head seems to have been a magical symbol to ward off evil long before the Perseus legend. Poseidon's love, 'and her name, which means "ruler", suggest that she was once an earth mother in the form of a horse from a version of the succession myth in which Poseidon was the chief god'. (John Pinsent, *Greek Mythology*, page 75)

This would make sense because Pallas Athene, though unquestionably a goddess (if almost the only utterly celibate one in the Classical Greek pantheon), time and again played an active role in the patriarchalization process, from her birth fully armed from the head of Zeus (who had swallowed her pregnant mother Metis) onwards. No wonder that she was his favourite child. She brooked no competition from older matriarchal goddesses, as many myths show (such as that of Arachne, who dared to compete with her in a weaving contest, and because of her success was turned into a spider). It may be that she herself was a development of an earlier matriarchal goddess, who could not be ousted from Athenian devotion even in patriarchal times, so was adapted accordingly on the principle of 'if you can't beat them, join them'. Her rivalry with Poseidon is a constant theme, beginning with their competition for the patronage of Athens – which in order to win she offered him the horse and the Athenians the olive tree. This is interesting to note from the point of view of our subject.

Another important creature based on the horse in Greek mythology was of course the centaur. He seems to have been born when the mounted tribes invaded Greece from Asia, and impressed upon the imagination of its indigenous horseless peoples the novel and awe-inspiring picture of man and beast acting as one being, with a single purpose and apparently complete harmony of action. This concept was perfectly represented by the centaur, a horse's body blended with a man's trunk, head and arms.

The accepted legend in Classical times made the centaurs wild hill-dwellers of Thessaly, with a reputation for drunkenness and lustfulness. They were related to the more civilized Lapiths of the same region, being the offspring of the Lapith king Ixion and a cloud replica of Hera which Zeus had made to divert his attention from Hera herself. At the wedding of Ixion's father Pirithous, the centaurs got very drunk and tried to carry off the women, including the bride Hippodamia (another form of the 'horse-tamer' name). This led to a war which the Lapiths won – a conflict finely portrayed on the Elgin Marbles from the Parthenon, now in the British Museum.

Thessaly is in the north of the Greek mainland, one of the directions from which the mounted invasion must have come; so perhaps the story of the Lapiths' victory was a memory of a temporarily successful frontier resistance to the onslaught. Or it may encapsulate the gradual transfer from the terrors of horse-born invasion to the integration of the horse into Mediterranean culture as an asset to peaceful activity. The Thessalian tribes were cattle-breeders, and the settling down of the invaders to the same activity is hinted at in the fact that the word centaur means 'he who rounds up bulls'.

This development from fear to ultimate integration is confirmed by the fact that early portrayals of the centaurs made them savage and lustful – an understandable reaction to the typical behaviour of conquerors. Later images (as in the Elgin Marbles), however, were more dignified.

Artists throughout history have been fascinated by the challenge of portraying centaurs, including Rubens, the nineteenth-century German painter, painter Arnold Bucklin, and Michelangelo himself, whose first sculpture, *The Battle of the Centaurs*, portrays the battle which arose from Pirithous' wedding.

In Ancient Greece, despite initial reluctance, the centaurs' cleverness was respected, and Chiron, the most famous of them, was seen as a model of wisdom.

Chiron's origins were reinterpreted accordingly. He had earlier been a Titan, son of Cronus and the ocean nymph Philyra, and thus the half-brother of Zeus himself. In his Titan form, he had dared to rebel against the Olympians, and was punished by Apollo turning into a monster, half man, half horse. In the respectable image he gradually acquired, he retained the same parentage, but was said to be skilled in many arts, from archery to medicine, and to have been the teacher of a number of heroes, including Achilles, Herakles, Asclepius, Castor, Polydeuces, Actaeon, and Jason, all of whom served an apprenticeship with him in the wilderness – and even of the historical Alexander the Great.

When his good friend Herakles accidentally wounded him with a poisoned arrow, Chiron gave up his immortality to

Prometheus (also a Titan), and as a reward for this unselfishness Zeus put him in the sky as the constellation Sagittarius.

Greek peasants still tell of the kallikantzaroi, 'good centaurs', hooved shaggy creatures who come out of the ground on winter nights. 'Good' is a propitiatory adjective, for they have a reputation for mischief, much like the Irish Puca who often takes the shape of a black horse.

A sub species of centaur were the centaur-Tritons, offspring of Poseidon (also a half-brother of Chiron) and his wife Amphitrite. They were a mixture of man and fish, with horses' legs, and they frisked in the sea around Amphitrite's chariot alongside her other children, the merman Tritons and the charming Nereid sea-nymphs.

The centaurs' original reputation for drunkenness survived in the frequent portrayal of them drawing the chariot (or being part of the entourage) of the wine god Dionysus, and perhaps indirectly in the Sileni, rollicking companions of Dionysus, who were shown with horses' hooves and tail, and sometimes their ears as well.

Whatever the historical origins of such concepts as the centaur, part human and part animal, their survival in human thinking is due to their psychological significance. As Tom Chetwynd puts it (*A Dictionary of Symbols*, p.17):

> The fusion of animals – or animals and men – indicates that the different parts have not been clearly distinguished. For example, the upper half, the conscious ego, may have been humanized, but the feelings (fish and horses) are still primitive, irrational and in need of conscious attention. But these figures remain joined to, therefore related to, their instincts and so have something vitally important to offer ... The fact that the human and animal parts are inseparably linked, is also meaningful.

Chiron, the wise flowering of the originally crude centaur concept, would thus symbolize the successful harmonization of the conscious and the instinctive.

Last of the pagan fabulous horse-creatures to consider is the unicorn. Its origins are quite different from those of the centaur, and so is its strange survival into comparatively modern times.

The first stories of it arose quite naturally from travellers' tales of several different animals, including the rhinoceros and various kinds of goat, ram, or antelope – especially those which look single-horned in profile.

The earliest surviving written mention of the unicorn in the west is that by the Greek historian Ctesias of Cnidos, who was court physician to the kings of Persia. Around 398 BC he wrote a book on India, and described a wild ass as being as big as a horse or bigger, white-bodied and red-headed, with a single horn about a foot and a half in length, white at the root, black in the middle, and crimson at the point. (Robert Graves, in *The White Goddess*, p.410, reminds us that white, red and black are the traditional colours of the Triple Goddess – Maid, Mother and Crone respectively.) Ctesias claimed that this horn, either powdered or formed into a drinking cup, was an effective protection against poison.

Rhinoceros horns, painted white, black and red, were used as drinking cups in India, and the Himalayan antelope does look single-horned when seen sideways. Persia had trade contacts with India, so Ctesias may well have seen a rhinoceros drinking horn and heard muddled tales of wild asses and antelopes.

Aristotle, and the Roman writers Pliny and Aelian, all gave their own descriptions of the unicorn, also from travellers' tales. The creature was said to be solitary and impossible to capture – which the rhinoceros certainly was. Oryx horn was easier to get, and was sold in Mediterranean lands as 'unicorn's horn'.

'In Britain, however, the narwhal horn became the accepted type, because of its white colour and superior hardness and because it is curved in the spiral of immortality' (Graves, ibid, p.410).

This patchwork picture of the unicorn was, of course, believed to be factual zoology (though the travelling salesmen who marketed 'unicorns' horns' may have been more cynical). Gradually, however, it entered into myth, and as it did so, it became standardized as equine. Though tales of the ass-unicorn also persisted, Herodotus accepted it as real.

The unicorn was international. Ancient Persian mythology was rich with its stories. It was a royal symbol in Ethiopia where its home was believed to be on the Mountains of the Moon, and it appears again and again in Buddhist art.

The Chinese unicorn was known as the *ki–lin*, from *ki* ('male') and *lin* ('female'). Like the *yin–yang* symbol, it represented the perfect balance of male and female qualities. Legend says it appeared to the mother of Confucius while she was pregnant with him, and that as an omen of the sage's death a charioteer accidentally injured a unicorn.

In the west, the admired characteristic of the horse which the unicorn typified was its solitary untameable freedom, seen as an essence of purity. This idea was emphasized in its central myth – that it was too fast and untamed to be caught by hunters, and could only be captured by a virgin.

The virgin had to sit down by herself under a tree, and the unicorn, sensing a purity akin to its own, would come and lay its head in her lap. In some versions, the virgin behaves surprisingly shabbily – lulling the beast to sleep, then breaking off its horn and calling the hunters to despatch it.

Other versions have erotic overtones, with both virgin and unicorn behaving in a definitely unvirginal manner.

The hunting of the unicorn appears in medieval folklore versions of the Grail legend, which overlap with stories of the quest for the philosophers' stone. Wolfram von Esenbach's thirteenth century epic *Parzival*, in which the Grail is not a cup but a jewel, contains the following stanza (Book IX, line 1494ff.):

> We caught the beast called Unicorn
> That knows and loves a maiden best
> And falls asleep upon her breast;
> We took from underneath his horn
> The splendid male carbuncle stone
> Sparkling against the white skull-bone

The unicorn also appears in Hindu tradition – even the virgin-and-unicorn theme. One story tells how a hermit named Rishyasyringa ('gazelle's horn'), son of Vibhandaka or Ekasringa ('one-horn'), is brought out of retreat by Shanta, the king's daughter, who marries him. In another version, he is seduced by a courtesan. Only thus can the terrible drought which is afflicting the land be broken.

Alleged unicorns' horns, known as alicorns, fetched high prices in the Middle Ages, for they still had the reputation of being an antidote to poison, and were thus obviously the safest thing to drink from. As late as the eighteenth century in France, supposed unicorns' horns were used to test the royal food for poison.

A horn said to be a unicorn's, and valued at £100,000, was exhibited in Windsor Castle in the Tudor period.

In early Christian times, an odd accident had happened. The Greek translators of the Bible rendered the Hebrew word *re–em* as monoceros – single-horned. In fact, as modern research has established, the *re–em* was the giant aurochs which had become extinct in the Middle East about 500 BC The mistake was repeated in the King James Authorized Version, which became and remained the definitive scripture of the English-speaking world; in that text it became 'unicorn'.

So the unicorn was in the Bible – in Numbers, Deuteronomy, the Psalms, Job, and Isaiah. To doubt its existence was to doubt Holy Writ. (The much later Revised Version got it right with 'wild ox', but by then believed-in myth had degenerated into mere fairy-tale.)

The unicorn was thus given, by a chance mistranslation, a new lease of life and a respectable passport.

The Talmud also contains Unicorn tales, based on the same misunderstanding of the word *re–em*.

Oddly enough, in view of its later heraldic use, the Talmud links the Unicorn with the lion, but as enemies:

> And in our land there is also the unicorn, which has a great horn on its forehead. And there are also many lions. And when the lion sees

a unicorn it draws him against a tree, and the horn pierces so deep into the tree it cannot pull it out again, and then the lion comes and kills the unicorn – but sometimes the matter is reversed.

Belief in the unicorn was universal. Even Leonardo da Vinci, perhaps the greatest combination of scientific and artistic genius of the Renaissance, made a special study of it and wrote that it could only be captured by a virgin.

The British Isles had only one native mythological one-horned beast – the Baiste-na-scoghaigh of Skye – but it was a great lumbering creature which was very different from the graceful imported unicorn.

(Two continental beasts that it would be a pity not to mention, even though they were not equine in form, were the bicorne, who devoured henpecked husbands and thus was happy with plenty to eat, and the chichevache, who fed on obedient wives and was therefore always half-starved!)

One popular belief was that the unicorn could determine whether a liquid was poison by dipping his horn in it and, if it was, could neutralize the poison by sipping from it. A gold and silver cup made by Ottavio Strada for the emperor Rudolph II depicts a unicorn placed as though it is about to test the cup's contents.

The unicorn was one of the supporters of the royal coat of arms of Scotland. James IV had unicorns as the supporters in his coat of arms, and the Scottish royal house retained these up to and including Mary Queen of Scots. When James VI of Scotland became James I of England, he added the unicorn to the royal arms of the unified kingdom, replacing the Red Dragon of Wales which had been introduced by Henry VII.

The pairing of the lion and the unicorn would not have been unfamiliar. Jung tells us: 'Medieval tradition associates the unicorn with the lion "because this animal is as strong, wild and cruel as the lions".' (*Collected Works Vol. 12*, p.437)

Both animals, Jung points out, were symbols of Mercurius in alchemy. He suggests that it is the single horn of the unicorn which is its key symbol.

> 'The unicorn is not a single, clearly defined entity but a fabulous being with a great many variations; there are, for instance, one-horned horses, asses, fish, dragons, scarabs etc. Therefore, strictly speaking, we are more concerned with the symbol of the single horn (the alicorn). In the Chymical Wedding of Rosenkreutz, a snow-white unicorn appears and makes his obeisance before the lion ... A little further on in the book the unicorn gives place to the white dove, another symbol of Mercurius, who, in his volatile form of spiritus, is a parallel of the Holy Ghost.'
>
> (Ibid. pp.436-7)

These changes underline the dual nature of the alchemical concept Mercurius, and of the unicorn itself – strength bordering on ruthlessness on the one hand, and incorruptible purity on the other.

Tom Chetwynd (*A Dictionary of Symbols*, p.412) suggests that the unicorn represents the inner world of mind and imagination, while the lion stands for the ordinary extrovert life of the ego. He goes on: 'The King was traditionally a mediator between these two realms' – which would make the two symbols appropriate supporters for the Royal arms.

On the well-known nursery rhyme about the lion beating the unicorn all around the town, Chetwynd adds: 'Depicts symbolically the fairly common situation, where society tries to get rid of tension, not by finding balance and equilibrium, but by repression. In the nursery rhyme the whole conflict is drummed out of town, i.e. into the unconscious, where it has been causing no end of social problems ever since.'

The unicorn entered into English slang in an odd way. In the eighteenth century, 'unicorn' was used to describe a three-horse carriage or coach with a leader in front and a pair behind him. Up to about 1870, the word was also used to mean two men and a woman, or two women and a man, working criminally together – doubtless a development of the earlier metaphor.

Christianizations of the unicorn-and-virgin legend included one which called it an allegory of Jesus Christ, who willingly became man and entered the Virgin's womb, and the Unicorn's single horn was said to symbolize Christ's oneness with God. Notwithstanding this, however, and other Christian rationalizations of the myth (some of them decidedly clumsy), and the mistranslation which accidentally included it in the Bible, the unicorn was, and remains, an essentially pagan beast.

IV *Horse Gods and Goddesses*

It is all too easy for Christians, Jews and Moslems to dismiss the animal God – and Goddess – forms of other faiths (whether contemporary or historical) as evidence of the primitive and barbaric nature of those faiths. This is in fact quite unjust.

Might not a visitor from another planet, for example, be forgiven for assuming that the Christians worshipped a sheep and a pigeon – or if you prefer the more usual words, a lamb and a dove? Christians would, of course, rightly protest at such an assumption.

The fact is that such animal forms, whether pagan or Christian, are symbolic. They may stand for a quality admired by a culture (or by its dominant class), and the particular animal symbols chosen depend on that culture's history, customs, environment and preoccupations.

The Christian symbols of the lamb and the dove, for instance, derive from the temple-sacrifice animals of the pre-Christian Hebrew religion from which Christianity stemmed. Both originally symbolized the spotless sacrifice, so it is understandable that Christ's early followers should adopt such ready-made and vivid symbols from the culture of their birth. The spotless-sacrifice meaning of the lamb remained unchanged, though the dove's symbolism moved in the direction of expressing the Holy Spirit alighting from above (for example, in the baptism of Jesus) and the concept of peace (perhaps because of its gentle soothing voice).

As for those cultures which adopted the horse as their divine symbol, it expressed the qualities of intelligence, wide-ranging mobility, beauty, strength, fertility, agility, sure-footedness – all virtues which one naturally attributes to deity. The horse had one thing in common with deity – the more one understood it, worked with it, and attuned oneself to its nature, the better friend and helper it became.

An additional element which enhances the symbology of the horse is that it encapsulates the valued qualities of both sexes. The stallion is unmistakably potent, actively energetic, defensive of the herd's safety, and unhesitating in his decisions. The mare is fertile, watchful, and capably nourishes and protects her young. Together, they vividly symbolize the fruitful and complementary polarity of gender.

On the female aspect – the horseshoe is often a symbolical representation of the female genitals. It is still the conventional figure for the Yoni in Hindu temples. As a charm against evil magic, it has an obvious similarity to the Sheila-na-Gig, the squatting naked female figure thrusting forward her enlarged genitals, which is found on many medieval Irish churches. The Sheila-na-Gig's purpose was the same – to frighten away evil spirits from the church door.

One quality of which the ancients were doubtless aware, and which for them may have added to the symbolism of the horse, is its capacity for all-round vision because of the placing of its eyes.

There may also have been people, even in tougher centuries, who respected the fact that horses (while they could fight when necessary) were herbivores, not needing to prey on other animals to keep themselves alive. A very appropriate deity-symbol, whether for Gods or Goddesses, one must admit.

One must also admit that warlike nations have always taken it for granted that God is on their side (a concept far from dead in Christendom, too). So nations or cultures which owed their success in conquering others to the horse (like the Manchus, the Mongols, and the Dorian Greeks) had an extra reason for regarding it as a symbol of 'their' deities.

There was often a class reason, too. In those cultures where the horse was a monopoly of the ruling caste (such as the Scandinavians), the mounted aristocrat never doubted for a moment that he was naturally superior to, and in command of, the unmounted peasant. The only superior he himself acknowledged was his God (or Gods); so he would instinctively attribute the same symbol of authority to Him (or Them).

Perhaps the earliest horse images of all (symbolically, if not chronologically) in western mythology come from the Chaldaeans. Their oldest deity was Tiamat, goddess of the original Chaos, the primordial bitter sea from which all life arose. She created unceasingly and experimentally, producing what would later be mankind's surrealist dream-images. Among these first attempts were horses with the snouts of dogs, and centaur-like creatures combining the hindquarters of a horse and the entire body of a man.

Among the later more specialized Chaldaean deities which evolved out of Tiamat's Chaos was Allat (whose name is the feminine form of Allah), who with her consort Nergal ruled over the Land of Aralu, the Underworld. She made a more practical, if unconventional, use of the horse, which by now had its proper image. 'According to the descriptions of her ... Allat passes through her empire, not seated, but standing on the back of a horse, which seems oppressed by her weight' (Lawrence Durdin-Robertson, *The Goddesses of Chaldaea, Syria and Egypt*, p.73).

A near eastern deity who was the lady of horses and chariots was the Phoenician ruling Goddess Astarte or Ashtart, who overlaps with (and was really the same as) the Assyrian Ishtar, and who appears in the Bible as Ashtoreth. She was also doubtless related to Isis (whose Egyptian name was Aset), and she seems to have been the source of the Teutonic Spring Goddess Eostre who gave her name to Easter.

The Greek Artemis (and her Roman equivalent Diana) included the horse among her totem animals. Her fellow Olympian Poseidon, God of the sea, was particularly symbolized by the horse – whether in its normal form, or in the fantasy form of half-horse, half-fish. Poseidon at least in his Classical form, seems to have been brought to Greece by the invading (horse-riding, Indo-European) Dorians, so it is not so surprising as it may, at first, seem that a Sea God should have such a land creature as his totem animal.

He would originally have been purely a horse God, acquiring his marine aspect as the invaders came to terms with the sea, with which most of them would have been as unfamiliar as the aboriginal inhabitants of Greece were with the horse. The sea was of such importance, however, to the settling invaders that they would have had to attribute it to one of their own major deities, which their horse God obviously was and, in due course, in the new environment, his acquired aspect became the major one.

When Pallas Athene won the patronage of Athens in competition with Poseidon, the Athenians not only built her temple on the Acropolis, they also diplomatically built one to Poseidon on Cape Sounion, a few miles outside their city so that he should not feel too rejected. When Janet and her husband were visiting Greece, they took a coach trip to Cape Sounion, and while the guide was telling the story of Athene and Poseidon, they noticed the coach driver touching a toy horse which dangled inside his windscreen for good luck – so it would seem the Athenians' diplomatic propitiation of Poseidon still persists.

Among the other Greek deities, Demeter, the Barley Goddess of fertility, and Hecate, Goddess of sorcery and of crossroads, were both sometimes portrayed with horses' heads.

Interestingly, the only occasion on which Poseidon (who was notoriously promiscuous) succeeded in seducing Demeter was when both were in horse form. She had turned herself into a mare and hidden herself among the horses of Oncios the Arcadian, in an attempt to avoid Poseidon's attentions. But the Sea God took on the form of a stallion and covered her. From this union were born a daughter whose real name was kept secret but who was simply referred to as Despoena, 'the mistress', and was much worshipped in Thessaly, and a wild horse called Arion, whose right feet were those of a man and who had the power of speech.

The Gaullish God Cunobelin (another form of Cernunnos or Herne) was portrayed with a Sun face. He too, like most Gods with solar attributes, was closely associated with the horse.

Svantovit (Swietovit) was a Slavonic God of the Island of Rugen in the Baltic. In his sanctuary were kept a bridle and saddle for his white horse, which only his priest was allowed to mount.

In Japanese mythology, the Goddess who produced the horse was Ukemochi-No-Kami, the Food Goddess. It was she who gave birth to all those good things which mankind needed: from her head, the horse and the ox, millet from her forehead, silkworms from her eyebrows, panic grass from her eyes, rice from her belly, and wheat and beans from her genitals. She produced all these at the command of the supreme deity, the Sun Goddess Amaterasu (whose symbol forms the present Japanese national flag).

To come to our own islands. The outstanding deity whose symbol was the horse was the Celtic Goddess Epona. Originally Gaullish, she was imported to Britain during the Roman occupation – without any difficulty because her attributes already overlapped with such native goddesses as Rhiannon.

Epona, 'the Divine Mare' (the name is related to the Greek word hippos ('horse'), was not envisaged as being herself equine; the horse was, rather, her totem animal. The famous White Horse of Uffington – the huge figure of a running horse cut in the chalk of the Berkshire hills – is believed by some to have been concerned wih her worship. Tradition still holds it to be lucky to stand within its eye and wish. Some people think that another hill-cut figure, at Wandlebury Camp near Cambridge, and generally called Magog, is in fact a mounted Epona. (Gog and Magog were said by Geoffrey of Monmouth to be giants whom Brutus made gatekeepers of London, but they seem originally to have been a God and his Goddess wife or mother and deities of a horse cult.)

Apart from these hill-figure possibilities, we have more unquestioned reliefs and statues of Epona than we do of other Celtic deities, for an odd reason. She caught the imagination of Roman cavalry units stationed in Celtic areas, and they adopted her as their patroness, taking her with them to other parts of the Empire. So we find portrayals of Epona in the stables of Roman forts in Britain, France, the Rhineland, and the Danube valley. She is portrayed mounted side-saddle, or lying half-naked along a horse's back, or standing between two or more of them. Her warlike aspect is sometimes expressed by her association in Gaul, and in cavalry barracks, with the Roman Mars.

She was even the only Celtic deity to be honoured in Rome itself; normally the Romans merely identified a Celtic deity with one of their own (Sucellos or the Dagda with Dis Pater, Thor with Jupiter, and so on), and renamed them accordingly. But Epona alone they honoured under her own name, as Epona Augusta or Epona Regina, and invoked her on behalf of the Emperor. She had a shrine in the barracks of the equites singulares, the mounted Imperial bodyguard, which was recruited mainly from Batavians.

Her mythology spread abroad with her. It is from a late Greek writer, Agesilaos, that we learn that she herself was born of a mare. He wrote: 'Phoulouios Stellos, who hated women, had relations with a mare. In time she gave birth to a beautiful little girl whom she named Epona.' Having thus the power of speech and choice, the mare was presumably a divine one.

(Epona could ride anything, apparently. In the north British kingdom of Brigantia, she sometimes rode a horned goose through the sky, scattering its feathers to make snowstorms. In this role, she was the origin of the pantomime *Mother Goose*.)

Epona was in fact just one form of the original Celtic great Mother Goddess, who developed over the centuries into several local forms such as the Irish Dana or Anu, the Welsh Dôn or Modron, and the more widespread lady who was known as Brighid (pronounced 'Breed') in Ireland, as Brigantia in Britain, as Brigindo in Gaul, and elsewhere on the Continent as Brigan or Brig. As well as her horse associations, Epona shared with all these Great Mother forms the aspect of fertility. She is often shown carrying a sheaf of corn, a cornucopia, or a goblet, and accompanied by birds (symbols of the Happy Otherworld – compare the Birds of Rhiannon, p.58), or holding a serpent (symbol, among other things, of sexual potency). In other portrayals she carries a key or a whip – presumably symbolizing her power to unlock the gates of life and fruitfulness, and her chastisement of transgressors, respectively. The Divine Mare was indeed an all-round goddess.

Talking of the Happy Otherworld – its Irish goddess was the outstandingly beautiful Cliodna, who presided over its favourite pastime, horse-racing.

Many other Irish goddesses were associated with horses. One of them was even so named – Étain Echraide which means 'Horse-riding Étain'. She symbolized the concept of reincarnation.

The name of the ancient capital of Ulster, Émain Macha, means 'Twins of Macha'. Macha, wife of Crunnchu, had to race there against the fastest horses in the land when she was pregnant, and died at the winning post giving birth to twins. In fact Macha was a battle goddess, patroness of warlike Ulster and like so many Irish deities, she became transmuted in Christian times into a legendary human, but in her story the equine links of the battle goddess survive.

The Goddess of Sovereignty aspect, which we mentioned previously, appears in another Irish goddess-turned-woman – the legendary Medhbh (Maeve, the Queen Mab of fairytale), Queen of Connacht. Until the chosen leader had slept with her, he was not King. Here, too, the divine mare recurs – Medhbh, like Macha, could outrun the fastest horse.

Lugh, the outstanding Young God figure in the Irish pantheon, was honoured annually in the Tailtean Games, halfway beween Navan and Kells in County Meath – a festival which survived into medieval times, and which featured a great deal of horse-racing. (The Gaelic name for August, *Lunasa*, means 'Festival of Lugh'.) There is still much interesting equine folklore in the area, as we shall see in Chapter VIII.

Horse associations were not confined to land gods. Manannán mac Lir, the Irish and Manx sea god (after whom the Isle of Man is named), rode a famous horse called Splendid Mane. ('Mac Lir', of course, means 'Son of Lir', and Lir was the original of Shakespeare's King Lear.)

The Welsh Happy Otherworld goddess was Rhiannon ('Great Queen'); her totem animal, like the Irish Cliodna's, was a mare. She could ride a white horse faster than any man could catch her, though always seeming to go at a steady pace (an image which appears to suggest, as with so many goddesses, lunar connections). She was in many ways a Welsh form of Epona.

A strange legend is told of Rhiannon from which, as Murry Hope suggests (*Practical Celtic Magic*, p.103): 'we may surmise that there was a period when the followers of the Horse Cult were badly treated, perhaps even persecuted. But in the aftermath of what was considered to be some supernatural occurrence or miracle, faith in the integrity of the Goddess was restored and the people turned to her once again.'

The legend tells how when Rhiannon was pregnant by her first husband, Pwyll (born a mortal, but by his marriage to Rhiannon became king of the Underworld), she delivered a boy child so painfully that she and all her ladies fell asleep. When the ladies awoke, the child had vanished. Fearing Pwyll's anger, the ladies killed a newborn staghound, laid its bones by Rhiannon, and smeared her face with its blood. When she awoke, they told her she had eaten her own child.

Pwyll believed the story, to which all the ladies swore, and punished Rhiannon by making her sit by the horse block at the castle gate, tell the story to any passer-by, and offer to carry him into the castle on her back. She did this for half a year.

Nearby lived Tiernyon of Gwent Is Coed who owned a beautiful mare. This mare foaled every May Day night, but the foal always vanished. One May Day Tiernyon stayed by the mare to solve the mystery. A handsome colt was born, but while Tiernyon was admiring it a clawed arm reached through the stable window and grabbed it. He cut off the arm with his sword, and ran outside, but whatever creature the arm belonged to had vanished, wailing as it went.

Back in the stable Tiernyon found beside the colt a boy child, wrapped in satin. His childless wife reared the lad, and they called him Gwri of the Golden Hair. He grew incredibly fast, and rode the colt that grew with him, with great skill.

Then Tiernyon heard the story of Rhiannon's punishment, and realized that Gwri was remarkably like Pwyll in features. So he and his wife decided they must take him to Pwyll's castle.

There they found Rhiannon at the gate, and she, as her punishment required, offered to carry them in. They would not let her, but showed her Gwri and declared he must be her missing son; her attendant ladies had lied. Everyone recognized his likeness to Pwyll, and Rhiannon said 'If this be true, there is an end to my trouble.' Pwyll realized that he had been lied to, and reinstated Rhiannon. The boy was thereafter called Pryderi ('Trouble').

Rhiannon was later more harmoniously married to Manawyddan ap Llyr (the Welsh equivalent of Manannán mac Lir). 'Her marriage to Pwyll representing no doubt some "troublesome" period when her cult was banished to the underworld or forced to go underground until it was re-established through the enchantments of Manawyddan at a later date'. (Murry Hope, ibid. p.103).

The Welsh Otherworld was called Annwn, and its god was Arawn. He too rode a pale-coloured horse, and led a pack of red-eared hounds in pursuit of a stag. There was a certain ambivalence about Annwn – in general it, and its equivalent in other Celtic lands, was regarded as a happy place. Pwyll's lordship of it may represent a more negative attitude during the 'troublesome' period Murry Hope postulates.

Horse symbolism accompanies Rhiannon's legends throughout. It was she who brought Pwyll to Annwn, not the other way round. She first came to seek his love mounted on a white horse. 'This is the image of the goddess of the Other World, the fairy in love with a mortal, whom she comes to carry off into the land of eternal youth ... The horsewoman is an image not only of death but of resurrection, since she comes from the night on a horse the colour of daylight.' (Jean Markale, *Women of the Celts*, p.88). The birth of her son, and her unjust punishment as a beast of burden, continue to identify her with the mare.

Also associated with Rhiannon were her birds – 'the birds of Rhiannon, which bring the dead back to life and put the living to sleep.' A perfect description of the magic of the Happy Otherworld which she ruled, and other Otherworld goddesses (such as Epona, as we have seen) had birds accompanying them.

Another Welsh deity famous for his swift horse-riding was Mabon, son of the goddess Modron ('Great Mother'). He seems to have represented the seasonally withdrawn fertility of the Earth, rather like the Greek Persephone.

We have already mentioned the probable horse-cult origins of the allegedly human Hengist and Horsa. Another British god was Herne, a horned God of Nature, who (not unlike Arawn) rode his steed at the head of the Wild Hunt of ghostly red-eyed hounds streaming through the night. Tradition says that he may sometimes still be seen in Windsor Great Park. His name seems to persist in such place-names as Herne Hill (often interpreted as 'Heron's Hill', but herons do not live on hills) and Cerne Abbas, site of the famous hill-figure giant who may in fact represent him. The interchangeability of H and K sounds is not uncommon in Celtic names – the Horned God name Cernunnos is doubtless another form of Herne.

Still in England – everyone knows the legend of Godiva, who rode naked on horseback through the streets of Coventry as a condition of her husband Leofric reducing the people's taxes, while out of loyalty to her the citizens (with the exception of Peeping Tom) stayed indoors behind closed shutters.

This story is in fact a monkish glossing-over of nearby spring rituals, a thousand years older than Leofric and Godiva, in honour of the goddess Goda. In hundreds of villages, May Day processions would be led by a woman enacting Black Annis, Hag of Winter, followed by a lovely girl representing Goda, Goddess of Spring and the rebirth of fertility, riding naked on horseback and not pretending to hide herself with her long hair – nor did the villagers, men or women, stay indoors. She was the female complementary symbol, in those less prudish days, to the phallic maypole.

Harold Bayley in his *Archaic England* links Godiva with Good Hipha, Hipha being the Tyrian title of the great mother goddess, whose name also meant 'mare'.

These processions were certainly attended by the whole community, male and female. There were elements, however, in the cult of the Celtic Goddess Brid, and of her successor St Bridget, which took place in sacred groves and were women's mysteries enacted by the Ingheana Adhanta (Daughters of Flame or Illumination) which no man might watch. Brid's English form was Brigantia, patroness of the kingdom of that name – and Coventry is in Brigantia territory. So it may well be that the Peeping Tom story recalls a man who dared to spy on such a mystery, and who had to be blinded by the Goddess in punishment for his sacrilege. Although the two rituals were originally distinct, they became merged in the folklore of the Godiva legend of Christian times.

Janet and Colin Bord (*Mysterious Britain*, p.160) wonder if the familiar nursery rhyme is a memory of a ritual procession of the Godiva type?

Ride a cock horse to Banbury Cross
To see a fine lady ride on a white horse;
Rings on her fingers, and bells on her toes,
She shall have music wherever she goes

A mysterious mounted deity is found on many monuments in the Balkans, especially in Thrace (the modern Bulgaria), dating from about the second and third centuries AD, and known as the

Thracian rider. Scholars are still uncertain who he was, or quite what qualities he represented.

He cannot have had a funerary significance, because he never appears on tombs. He does seem to represent the aspects of vigour and speed, because he is usually portrayed with his cloak streaming behind him. He sometimes brandishes a club or double axe – the latter being a symbol of many Near Eastern sky and weather gods. Quite often he appears with three heads, looking forwards, backwards, and straight ahead, which usually symbolizes an omniscient God, superhuman in his grasp of everything (frequently the attributes of a Sun deity). Sometimes he is shown hunting a great boar, which suggests a saviour deity who pursues and destroys evil.

He is seldom named. Those inscriptions which do give him a name, may call him 'the God Hero' (eliminating the possibility that he was a revered human), or Phoebus (God of the sun and enlightenment), or Asclepios (Greek God of healing).

No single one of these attributes can be said to predominate, either in his pictorial symbolism or in his occasional naming. The frequency of images of the Thracian Rider, however, make it quite clear that he had deep significance for the people of the area.

Not all equine deities were benevolent. The Irish Puca (Pooka) – a pre-Celtic god who degenerated into a mere malicious spirit – could take on many shapes, his favourite being that of a black horse. (His name is cognate with that of Shakespeare's mischievous Puck.) Also the Scottish kelpie, a spirit (doubtless originally a god) of lakes and rivers, often appeared in the form of a horse, and caused travellers to drown.

The pagan roots of the Basque people of south-western France and northern Spain run deep. Their supreme deity was (and to many secretly still is) the goddess Mari. Her totem animal, too, is the horse, and sometimes the heifer as well. She lives in the depths of the Earth, but is also lunar, liking to ride across the sky at night in a cart pulled by a four-horse team.

The Norse pantheon was a clear example of the class element

in horse symbolism. These gods and goddesses were common to the Scandinavians, the Germans, and the Anglo-Saxons, the deities' name-forms differing slightly with their location; but it is from the Scandinavian poets that we inherit the richest harvest of their legends.

Their chief god was originally the thunder god Thor (Thunor), after whom Thursday is named. He was the much-loved god of the peasants and local chieftains, and although a doughty warrior when the need arose, he was the patron of home, marriage, and the family. He and his pantheon were known as the Vanir. As centralized kingship developed, however, Thor was gradually outranked by Odin (Woden, Wotan), known as the all-father, god of the warrior aristocracy and of the king who regarded him as his ancestor. His pantheon was known as the Aesir. Odin, after whom Wednesday is named, was a god of intelligence, magic, law-giving, and war. Thor's demotion even took the form of his sometimes being called Odin's son.

Significantly, the peasant god Thor never rode horseback; when he did not use his own two feet, he travelled in a carriage drawn by two he-goats. The aristocratic Odin, on the other hand, rode a horse which outshone all others – the eight-legged grey Sleipnir ('Swift One'), who could carry him on land, across the sea, or through the air, and even to the Underworld realm of the goddess Hel.

Dag, the Norse god of day, rode a white horse called Shining Mane through the sky, its brightness illuminating the world, and Mani, the Moon goddess, travelled in a chariot drawn by Alsvidur, 'All-Swift.'

Important gods of the warrior-aristocracy pantheon all seem to have possessed named horses. For example, that of Heimdahl, guardian of the rainbow bridge Bifrost between Earth and Asgard, home of the gods, was called Culltoppr, while that of Gna, messenger of the gods, was Hofvarpnir.

Most important of the Aesir fertility deities were Frey (Freyr) and his sister Freyja, twin children of the sea and fertility god

Njörd. Horses were sacrificed to Frey, and the Icelandic saga of Hrafnkel, priest of Frey, tells of a horse dedicated to the god by its owner and which no man was allowed to ride. The ritual of horse sacrifice was so ingrained that when Hakon the Good, first Christian king of Norway, tried to avoid it, he was obliged to bow to popular custom and even had to eat the flesh and drink the blood of the sacrificed animal.

Among the Norsemen's Slav neighbours, equestrianism was much less class-conscious, as might be expected with peoples many of whom inhabited the vast steppes. Several of their deities, as one might also expect in such terrain, had horse associations.

Khors, a Slavonic god of health and hunting, was almost unique among Western deities in that the horse was not merely his totem animal; he was himself envisaged as a stallion.

Another hunting deity, on the more wooded western Slav fringe, was the goddess Devana (Diiwica to the Serbians of Lusatia, Dziewona to the Poles). Young and beautiful, she rode a swift horse through the forests of the Elbe and the Carpathians, leading a pack of hounds. Her name and attributes stemmed originally from the Roman Diana.

Also youthful and mounted was Yarilo, Slav god of passion, sexual love, and fertility. He was envisaged as white-clad, flower-crowned, and carrying a sheaf of corn. Like many fertility gods, he was regarded as seasonal; young girls held a flower festival to greet his rebirth in the spring, and in autumn his funeral rites were marked by dancing and feasting.

The god Triglav had four temples in Stettin. He was envisaged as three-headed, representing Heaven, Earth, and the Underworld, and all three faces were veiled so that he might not see the sins of the world. He had an oracular black horse from whose behaviour omens were read.

Many cultures have legendary sleeping heroes who will wake at the hour of their countries' need. Among the Serbs, it is Prince Marco, son of a dryad (tree nymph), who sleeps in a cave mounted upright on his horse. His sword is rising slowly from its sheath, and when it is fully drawn, Marco will awaken and ride forth to save his country from its enemies.

Horses are often an essential accompaniment to the Sleeping Heroes. One example from England is a strong local tradition at Alderley Edge. The Edge is a sheer sandstone cliff rising from the Cheshire plain. It has a wishing well bearing the inscription:

> Drink from this and take thy fill,
> For the water falls by the wizard's will.

The wizard is said to be Merlin himself. The local legend tells how a farmer taking a fine white mare to market for sale was stopped by the bearded old man, who offered to buy it. The farmer refused, hoping to get a better price at the market. Although many people admired the mare, however no one was prepared to make him an offer for it. On the way home, the disappointed farmer again met the wizard, who led him through the woods to a rock, which he touched. A huge pair of gates opened with a thunderous sound.

Inside, the wizard told the farmer, lay King Arthur and his knights with their horses, sleeping till England needed them. They were one white horse short, however. The wizard gave him a purse of gold for his mare, and the terrified farmer accepted it and ran out. The gates slammed shut behind him, and no one has seen the cavern since. The pub on the road running behind the top of the Edge is named The Wizard.

Another sleeping hero is the Moorish Alfatin, who rests in a cave in the Sierra de Agner, from which he will one day emerge to rescue his people. With him is his green horse – green being the colour both of Islam and, in that culture, of fairyland.

The greek sun god, Helios, traversed the sky in a chariot drawn by winged horses, who grazed between journeys on a magic herb in the Isles of the Blessed in the far west. His son Phaeton tricked Helios into allowing him to drive the solar chariot for one day – but only the true king or god can control the steeds which are the symbols of his sovereignty. Phaeton failed to do so, and died in the attempt.

In many mythologies, thunder was the sound of these heavenly horses' hooves, and lightning the flash of their divine drivers' whips.

The island of Rhodes (named after Rhode, who bore him seven children) was sacred to Helios, and every year its people would dedicate a chariot and four horses to him, and throw them into the sea for his use. Similar annual horse sacrifices to the Sun were practised by the early kings of Judah, the Spartans, the Persians, and the Massagetae.

The Greek Moon Goddess Artemis, and her Roman equivalent Diana, likewise rode the heavens in a horse-drawn chariot. The Roman poet Ovid expressed this image in his *Fasti*: 'When the next dawn shall have shone in the sky, and the stars have vanished, and the Moon shall have unyoked her snow-white steeds …' (*Fasti*, IV, 373).

Ovid's *Fasti* describe the various Roman festivals in honour of their gods and goddesses, and he gives several horse references. For example, in IV, 389 he tells how 'horses, fleet as the wind, will contend for the first palm' on the last day of the goddess Cybele's festival of Megalesia, 10 April. For 15 April, when Venus was said to hasten the sunset, he declares that she 'hurried the galloping [solar] horses downhill, that on the next day the youthful Augustus might receive the sooner the title of Emperor'. (Venus was said to be the divine ancestress of the Julian dynasty.)

Both the solar and the lunar horse themes are also found in Hindu tradition. Ushas, the Dawn goddess, 'leads the white and lovely steed of the Sun', and one of the twenty-seven Hindu lunar mansions is Asvayug, which means 'yoked with horses'.

Tibet, too, has a complex array of deities distributed round the compass – one of the western ones being the Red Horse-Headed Delight Goddess.

In Hindu belief Vishnu, supreme god of the Vedic pantheon,

has had many avatars (incarnations) on Earth, and it is said that for his tenth and final avatar, he will appear riding (or in the form of) a white horse amid fire and flames. The name Kalki seems to be used sometimes for himself in this avatar, and sometimes for the horse.

An earlier Vishnu incarnation, the Avatar of the Turtle, is involved with a popular Hindu legend – the Churning of the Milk Ocean. Several remarkable beings arose from this sea of milk, including Dhanvantari, doctor of the gods, and a miraculous Pegasus-type horse.

The ancient Hindu text *Brhad Aranyaka Upanishad* equates the various parts of the sacrificial horse with the elements of the universe:

> Dawn … is the head of the sacrificial horse. The Sun is his eye; the Wind his breath; the sacrificial Fire his open mouth; the Year is the body of the sacrificial horse. The Sky is his back; the Atmosphere, his belly; the Earth, his underbelly; the Directions, his flanks; the Intermediate Directions, his ribs; the Seasons, his limbs; the Months and Half-Months, his joints; Days and Nights, his feet; the Stars, his bones; the Clouds, his flesh. Sand is the food in his stomach; Rivers, his entrails; Mountains, his liver and lungs; Plants and Trees, his hair; the Rising Sun, his forepart; the Setting Sun, his hindpart. When he yawns, then it Lightnings; when he shakes himself, then it Thunders; when he urinates, then it Rains. Speech is actually his neighing.

Agni was the Hindu god of fire, and the sacrificial fire itself personified him. The *Rig Veda* (1500–1200 BC) contains the following hymn to him, in his horse form (English version by Robert Kelly):

> Your eyes do not make mistakes.
> Your eyes have the sun's seeing.
> Your thought marches terribly in the night
> blazing with light and the fire
> breaks from your throat as you whinny in battle.
> This fire was born in a pleasant forest
> This fire lives in ecstasy somewhere in the night.

His march is a dagger of fire
His body is enormous
His mouth opens and closes as he champs on the world
He swings the axe-edge of his tongue
smelting and refining the raw wood he chops down.

He gets ready to shoot and fits arrow to bowstring
He hones his light to a fine edge on the steel
He travels through night with rapid and various movements
His thighs are rich with movement.
He is a bird that settles on a tree.

On the other side of the world, an American Indian extolled his horse in similar poetic terms. This was interpreted into English by Louis Watchman, and published in 1930 by Dane and Mary Roberts Coolidge in their book *The Navaho Indians*:

I am the Turquoise Woman's son.
On top of Belted Mountain
beautiful horses – slim like a weasel!
My horse with a hoof like a striped agate,
with his fetlock like a fine eagle plume:
my horse whose legs are like quick lightning
whose body is an eagle-plumed arrow: my horse whose tail is
like a trailing black cloud.
The Little Holy Wind blows thru his hair.
My horse with a mane made of short rainbows.
My horse with ears made of round corn.
My horse with eyes made of big stars.
My horse with a head made of mixed waters.
My horse with teeth made of white shell.
The long rainbow is in his mouth for a bridle
and with it I guide him.
When my horse neighs, different-coloured horses follow.
When my horse neighs, different-coloured sheep follow.
I am wealthy because of him.

Before me peaceful
Behind me peaceful
Under me peaceful
Over me peaceful –

Peaceful voice when he neighs.
I am everlasting and peaceful.
I stand for my horse.

Both these poems are published in Jerome Rothenberg's book *Technicians of the Sacred* (see Bibliography).

The other side of the horse symbology coin is that of the ass. In general, it implies humility – or at the negative extreme, the ridiculous and stubborn. There is something of all these in Lucius Apuleius's second-century classic *The Golden Ass*, in which the hero is turned into an ass to learn all his lessons (some serious and some hilarious), and is finally restored to human shape by his dedication to the goddess Isis.

One wonders whether Shakespeare had Lucius Apuleius in mind when he turned Bottom into an ass in *A Midsummer Night's Dream* – though this was pure comedy, and it is doubtful whether Bottom learned any lessons from it.

An extreme of the negative aspect was the Egyptian God, Set, who was represented as an ass. He stood for the destructiveness of the desert, permanently threatening the fertile Nile valley. In mythology, he was the ruthless enemy of the great Egyptian Holy Family of Isis, Osiris and Horus. By treachery he brought about the death of Osiris and cut him into pieces, which Isis had to reassemble and reanimate magically.

It is interesting that before the unification of Egypt, and the evolution of its integrated pantheon, Set was a Sun God of upper Egypt – and the horse is an archetypal symbol of a Sun God. So when Set became visualized as evil, perhaps it is not surprising that his animal symbol became that of the negative counterpart of the horse.

Set was also worshipped by the Hyksos invaders, which doubtless gave added emphasis to his demotion after their departure.

The outstanding example of the humility aspect of the ass is, of course, Jesus's ride to Jerusalem on its back. The ass's own reaction to this is touchingly and ironically imagined in G.K.

Chesterton's poem *The Donkey*, where 'the devil's walking parody of all four-footed things' ends by saying:

> Fools! For I also had my hour;
> One far fierce hour and sweet;
> There was a shout about my ears,
> And palms before my feet.

Memory of this may have inspired the legend of the Abbot Helenus and the wild ass. It is said the good abbot was carrying a heavy load of food and other comforts to some sick brethren across the desert, and was overcome with fatigue. Seeing a herd of wild asses in the distance, he called out: 'In the name of our Lord Jesus Christ, let one of you come here and take my pack!' One of them trotted over and joined him, and willingly carried him and his load for the rest of his journey.

In some folk customs, the smallness and manageability of the ass may enter into its significance. For example, it was believed that a child could be cured by passing it over and under the body of an ass.

Gypsies consider it bad luck to meet an ass on the road, but good luck to meet a white horse.

Just why the donkey (as they prefer to call it) became the symbol of the American Democratic Party, while the elephant became that of the Republicans, remains a mystery to us, as it does to an American friend we asked. He added: 'Maybe it was the only non-Masonic animal they could find!'

Horses, asses and zebras are biologically closely related, so closely in fact that they can interbreed. The zebra is probably the most similar in its physical characteristics to their common ancestors; some experts even believe that these ancestors may all have been striped for camouflage, though since fossils do not normally preserve natural colouring, this is difficult to prove. The wild asses of Somalia are striped on all four legs.

The ass was domesticated in the west long before the horse – the royal standard of Ur of the Chaldees (c.2000 BC) shows asses pulling chariots.

V *Biblical and Christian Lore*

Throughout the Bible, horses are exclusively warhorses which were principally used for drawing chariots. Palestine's hilly terrain confined even this use to certain areas.

They were not shod, so hard-hooved breeds were specially valued. The potential exploitation of horses by the ambitious was regarded with wariness, and even the king had to observe certain limitations, particularly in the period following the Exodus. Deuteronomy xvi 15–16 lays down:

> Thou shalt in any wise set him king over thee, whom the Lord thy God shall choose ... But he shall not multiply horses unto himself, nor cause the people to return to Egypt, to the end that he should multiply horses: forasmuch as the Lord hath said unto you, Ye shall henceforth return no more that way.

Solomon, a law to himself in many ways, seems to have ignored this rule: 'And Solomon had forty thousand stalls of horses for his chariots, and twelve thousand horsemen'. (I Kings iv 26).

The most poetical reference to the horse, however, which sums up vividly the Hebrew concept of it, is in Job xxxix 19–25:

> Hast thou given the horse his strength? hast thou clothed his neck with thunder?
> Canst thou make him afraid as a grasshopper? the glory of his nostrils is terrible.
> He paweth the valley, and rejoiceth in his strength; he goeth on to meet the armed men.

> He mocketh at fear, and is not affrighted; neither turneth he back from the sword.
> The quiver rattleth against him, the glittering spear and the shield.
> He swalloweth the ground with fierceness and rage; neither believeth he that it is the sound of the trumpet.
> He saith among the trumpets, Ha, ha; and he smelleth the battle afar off, the thunder of the captains, and the shouting.

Hebrew tradition says that Satan rebelled against God a week after the creation of Adam, declaring war on the hosts of the Almighty. The Satanic army charged with horses and chariots, and twice drove God's forces back. Finally God gave his army a cross of light, inscribed with the names of the Trinity. When Satan's forces saw this, they lost all their strength, men and horses alike, and Michael and the angels were able to drive them into Hell, where many Hebrews and Christians still believe they remain.

The Hebrew religious establishment was well aware of the symbolic importance of horses to many of their pagan neighbours, and was ready to pounce on any infiltration of their ideas. King Josiah, in his campaign against the 'heathen' practices rife in Judaea (II Kings xxiii) 'took away the horses which the kings of Judah had given to the sun ... and burned the chariots of the sun with fire' (verse 11). Mention of the sun emphasizes the religious significance of these horses, for horses in many religions embody solar symbolism.

Almost the only mention of a horse in a significant but non-military context is in Esther vi, when Queen Esther foils Haman's plot to frame her kinsman Mordecai as a traitor. King Ahasuerus signifies his royal favour by having Mordecai ride to court on a handsomely apparelled horse. Then the Book of Esther is an interesting oddity; it is completely pagan in origin – the only book in the Bible, apart from the Song of Solomon, which does not mention the Hebrew God. The name Esther, which the heroine Hadassah took upon her marriage, is a form of Ishtar, the title of the greatest of the Middle Eastern goddesses. The story is in fact yet another version of the mating of the king with the Goddess of Sovereignty, personified by her priestess, to validate his title.

During the Babylonian Exile, many Hebrews adopted their captives' customs and rituals, including the full moon festival of Ishtar which became the Jewish *Purim* (itself an Assyrian word). The Book of Esther as it appears in the Old Testament was written a few years BC, doubtless to make this festival, which was far too popular to suppress, as respectable as possible. So this uniquely non-military horse reference, of obvious symbolic importance in its context, must reflect Assyro-Babylonian rather than orthodox Hebrew tradition.

The most notable equine reference in the New Testament is that in Revelation vi 1–8 – the so-called Four Horsemen of the Apocalypse. All four confirm the Hebrew image of the horse as a symbol of war and destruction rather than as a means of peaceful travel, haulage, ploughing, or harmless sport.

The four are revealed, one by one, as the first four of the seven seals on the Book of Destiny are opened.

The first seal-breaking reveal a crowned archer riding a white horse, who 'went forth conquering, and to conquer'. He represents military victory. Some have identified the rider with Christ, or with the victorious Church, but this conflicts with the overall implication that the four are scourges which afflict mankind. It would seem more reasonable to accept the first horse and rider as symbolizing successful war and the human destruction it involves.

The second horseman carries a sword and rides a red horse, the colour of blood; to him is given the power 'to take peace from the earth, and that they should kill one another'. He represents slaughter, pure and simple.

The third rides a black horse, and carries a pair of scales; he represents famine. The text speaks of 'a measure of wheat for a penny, and three measures of barley for a penny; and see thou hurt not the oil and wine'. This apparently puzzling passage in fact refers to food shortage, when for example a man needed his whole day's wage (which averaged a denarius or 'penny') merely to buy enough cereal to keep himself alive – and never mind such luxuries as oil and wine.

The fourth rides a pale (or as the New English Bible translates it, 'sickly pale') horse. He is Death, the inescapable companion of the other three, 'and Hell followed with him'.

The four colours are appropriate: the white of proud victory, the red of spilled blood, the black despair of starvation, and the sickly pale of corpses.

It is not till the grim symbology of the four horsemen is dispensed with that the breaking of the remaining seals carries the hope of afterlife and salvation from the terrors that afflict humanity.

The name of St Hippolytus ('loosed horse'), a Roman said to have been martyred on 13 August 235 by being torn asunder by horses, is remembered in that of the village of Ippolitts in Hertfordshire. He must have forgiven his equine executioners, because sick horses used to be brought through the north door of Ippolitts church, and led to his shrine where they were touched with the relics of the saint to heal them, in exchange for a thank-offering.

St Hippolytus appears to have existed historically, because several of his writings are known. His legends, however, are interestingly intertwined wih those of the Greek legendary hero of the same name, beloved of the Goddess Artemis. This Hippolytus angered Aphrodite, and as a result was dragged to death by horses, and 13 August is the day of Artemis. As Sir James Frazer puts it (*The Golden Bough*, p.7), the Greek hero 'after dying twice over as a heathen sinner, has been happily resuscitated as a Christian saint'.

St Aldhelm (639–709), Abbot of Malmesbury in Wiltshire and Bishop of Sherborne in Dorset has a legend told of him which involves not only the casting of a magic circle, but the evocation of a winged horse.

When he was a simple monk at Malmesbury, he produced a little silver bell which could silence storms. Word of this travelled far, and when it reached Rome he was summoned by the Pope. The then Abbot was worried about how to get him there, but Aldhelm was untroubled. He drew a chalk circle on the floor, and forbade anyone to enter it or to touch anything that appeared in it.

The first thing to manifest was a strange dark shape which said it could take him to Rome 'as fast as a bird on the wing'. Not fast enough for Aldhelm, so he banished it and tried again.

The second manifestation was a white misty shape, which could take him to Rome 'as fleet as an arrow from a bow'. Aldhelm was still not satisfied.

The third shape he summoned was of flame, and promised to take him to Rome 'in the blink of an eye'. Aldhelm accepted its offer, and it turned into a winged white horse, already saddled and bridled. Its hooves struck fire as it moved.

Aldhelm mounted it, and in no time he was in Rome, where he led the horse through the streets to the Pope. During his audience, he left the horse with a groom, instructing him to feed it on live coals.

After nine days, he remounted his winged steed and returned to Malmesbury. The horse vanished, and Aldhelm never left England again.

St Martin appears on a white horse in a tradition from County Wexford. There used to be a taboo there against deep-sea fishing on Martinmas, 11 November. One year in the eighteenth century, however, there was a particularly rich shoal of herring off the Wexford coast, and the fishermen set sail on Martinmas, ignoring the ban. St Martin, it is said, materialized before them on the waves on his white mount, and warned them to return to harbour. Two of the boats obeyed him. The rest ignored his warning and carried on fishing – and every boat and all seventy men, the tradition maintains, were lost.

(Wexford, incidentally, is rich in pagan lore. Even the Gaelic name of the county, Lough gCarman, is after the local Goddess, Carman.)

A touching tale of equine sensitivity is told of St Columkille (known outside Ireland as St Columba) when he knew he was near to death. He was resting by the roadside with his servant Diarmid, when the white horse who used to carry their milk pails came up and started to mourn, weeping tears on to the saint's breast as a human might. Diarmid wanted to drive it away, but Columkille said: 'Behold, you that are a man and have a reasonable soul could in no way have known of my departing if I had not but now told you; yet to this dumb and irrational beast, his Creator in such fashion as pleased Him has revealed that his master is to go from him.' He then blessed the horse, and it went on its way.

The archangel Michael (whose name means 'like unto God') was, as we have seen, patron of horses and horsemen. This is not surprising, since as the commander of God's armies, he would often be envisaged on horseback. He was also associated with the element of fire, and this may well have echoed the fact that many pagan war gods were fire gods (with equine symbolism).

The earliest Christian missionaries to Britain were instructed by the Pope not to ban or destroy pagan holy places, but to take them over, so that people would continue to revere such places to which they were accustomed, but in Christian terms. As a result, the saint names of Christian churches were often chosen to fit the aspect already honoured there. Thus very many first-millennium churches of St Michael were built on sites once sacred to fire/war/equine pagan gods – particularly on high places, which is where fire gods were naturally worshipped.

(The other three traditional elemental associations of archangels, incidentally, were Auriel for earth, Raphael for air, and Gabriel for water. Gabriel is also sometimes envisaged as mounted; the Koran names his horse as Haizum.)

The pagan theme of horses being magically linked with their hero owners, often being born at the same time as in the case of Cuchulainn or Rhiannon's son, or being clairvoyant about their fate, persisted into medieval Christianity. For example, the white horse of the Irish St Columkille was said to have foreseen his beloved master's death on Iona, and to have shed bitter tears at the knowledge.

In medieval Christendom, the horse had officially lost its divine symbolism, but it remained a powerful symbol of the ruling class and of military success – two names for the same thing. The Normans were the most brilliant horsemen of their time; the most important factor in their military success was their mounted knights. Their mounts were very special. Draught horses would be too clumsy to manoeuvre, and palfreys unable to carry an armoured rider.

The anwer was the destrier, specially bred for manoeuvrability, speed and strength, and trained not to panic. It cost about thirty times as much as a palfrey, so knighthood was synonymous with wealth. It was also a lifelong calling; a ninth-century proverb said a horseman could be made of a lad at puberty, but later than that never.

English feudalism was founded, and ruled by, a Norman aristocracy descended from the mounted knights of the Conquest of 1066. So it was hardly surprising that the horse became the symbol of that rule.

Nor is it untypical that right up to the war of 1914–18, when an officer was automatically such because of his class, even in the infantry officers rode while 'other ranks' marched. (Officers' rank badges, up to that war, were on the cuffs where they could be seen from below, not on the shoulder epaulettes as they are now.) The tank, and accurate modern firearms, made this distinction impracticable on the battlefield, but it lingered for a while yet on the parade ground.

Up to about the seventeenth century, dancing was an accepted element of Christian ritual, as it had been of Old Testament Hebrew worship; and in France in the Middle Ages, young people were allowed to ride to church on wooden horses and dance in the churchyard, masked and disguised, on the eve of dedication day. The sterner Fathers frowned on such goings-on as an invention of the Devil and the occasion of frequent sin, and eventually managed to put a stop to them.

VI *The Magic of Smithcraft*

When the Iron Age swept across the Mediterranean and Europe during the last millennium BC it did so unevenly, some peoples mastering the new metal earlier than others, or having easier access to the ore. Such peoples became conquerors as a result. Their weapons were greatly superior; an iron sword cut deeply, while a bronze sword, however mightily wielded, depended on weight and momentum rather than on sharpness, and seldom did more than break bones and bruise flesh.

Of course, the conquering warriors' iron-shod horses gave them a further advantage.

Iron-smelting began in the Armenian Mountains some time between 1200 and 1000 BC. Wandering gypsies played a great part in spreading its use. 'The Gypsies were conspicuous as smiths as soon as they appeared in our civilization. The cauldron-makers of Corfu are remembered, and the shoeing-smiths who have been known in Serbia since the 14th century.' (Jean-Paul Clebert, *The Gypsies*, p.98.) The very name 'tinker' by which gypsies are widely known emphasizes their reputation as metalworkers.

The only iron which had been known to Stone and Bronze Age peoples before iron mining and smelting were introduced had been in the form of meteorites – lumps of a mysterious and miraculously hard substance flung from Heaven by the Gods, and flaming as they fell.

It was hardly surprising, therefore, that the men who had learned the secret of this divine metal, and harnessed it to human use – the blacksmiths – were regarded with awe by conquered and conquerors alike, and credited with magical powers. (The gypsies, among the earliest of them, already had such a reputation.) Nor is it surprising that smith Gods such as the Greek Hephaestos, the Roman Vulcan, the Irish Goibniu, the Welsh Govannon, and the Anglo-Saxon Volund/Wayland, ranked high in their respective pantheons – even if, as with Hephaestos, their powerful talents made the older Gods concede them rights with some reluctance (in Hephaestos's case, the hand of golden Aphrodite).

The human blacksmith's social standing was correspondingly high. His forge was normally at a crossroads near running water, and a natural rallying-point. 'Not being a food-producer he was, like the seers and later the priests, entitled to a tribute of corn and first fruits. When a beast was slain the head was the perquisite of the smith.' (E. Estyn Evans, *Irish Folk Ways*, p.199)

At a national or tribal level – the king or chief kept a jealous eye on so precious a craftsman. Often only the king had direct contact with him, other customers leaving a block of iron and a sum of money near the forge and collecting the finished product a few days later. In the Fan tribe of Central Africa, the two functions were combined; the chief was also smith and medicine man, these roles being too sacred for anyone but the chief to handle.

A story which underlines the value which rulers set upon capable smiths is told of Robert the Magnificent, Duke of Normandy (1027–35). A smith from Beauvais came to him with two knives, and recognizing their quality the Duke told his chamberlain to give the smith a hundred Rouen pounds. This generous payment astonished the smith – and he was still more amazed when he was sent two fine horses. He lingered at the court, but when he was finally reassured that the gifts were genuine, he rode home.

Told that the smith had gone, the Duke (who had more gifts ready) wondered why. 'If he had stayed a little, I would have made him among the rich and noble.'

The smith had not forgotten, however. A year later he brought the Duke his two sons, well trained in arms, 'to offer you faithful service, if Your Excellency will not refuse it'.

The belief in blacksmiths' magical powers persisted throughout history, and was confidently shared by blacksmiths themselves. Blacksmiths, for instance, were reputed to have the curative gift of stopping the flow of blood in people or animals.

A nineteenth century example of the blacksmith's reputation comes from Lady Gregory's book *Visions and Beliefs in the West of Ireland*. One smith, talking to her about the healing gifts of the famous County Clare witch Biddy Early, added: 'I never went to her myself – for you should know that no ill or harm ever comes to a blacksmith'.

Lady Gregory quotes other comments from Irish country people on the powers of smiths. 'If a blacksmith was to turn his anvil upside down and to say malicious words, he could do you great injury' ... 'Blacksmiths have power, and if you could steal the water from the trough in the forge, it would cure all things' ... 'As to forges, there's some can hear working and hammering in them through the night.'

The importance of the anvil for both cursing and healing, particularly for women, was enhanced by the fact that it was often even more of a meeting-place for them than the local pub. In many places, women were customarily not allowed into the bars, but the smith's forge would be both central and warm.

In the Kiltartan area of County Galway, it was believed that the blacksmith gave power to his curses by turning the anvil as he uttered them.

In north County Mayo, the smith's power to curse was believed to extend to anyone who was descended from a smith. One example of this concerned a girl who had been made pregnant by a man who refused to marry her. She took a way out which was common at the time – emigrating to America. Her sister, however, bent on family revenge, remembered that one of their ancestors was a blacksmith. So she cursed her sister's lover on the village blacksmith's anvil, turning it widdershins (anti-clockwise) as she did so. It is said that the man never had another day's luck in his life.

An eighth-century hymn known as St Patrick's Breastplate invokes God's protection against 'spells of women, smiths and druids' and 'all knowledge that is forbidden to the human soul'. Proinsias MacCana (*Celtic Mythology*. p.35) comments that this 'presents a jaundiced ecclesiastical view of this peculiar faculty and no doubt runs counter to general contemporary attitudes'. The greatest popular respect was for the smith's healing powers, rather than for any malignant magic, though one was of course wary of offending him. The Irish smith god Goibniu was also credited with therapeutic powers; a traditional old Irish charm, for instance, invokes his name for the removal of a thorn.

Blacksmiths had their own taboos. 'Blacksmiths in the nineteenth century often refused to shoe horses, or do any work with nails on Good Friday. The reason usually given was that nails must not be touched then because of the terrible use to which they had been put on Calvary.' (E. and M.A. Radford, *Encyclopaedia of Superstitions*, p.57)

Alcester in Warwickshire has a story about blacksmiths having magic turned against them for working on Sundays. Before the Norman Conquest, Alcester was an iron-working town. St Egwin, Bishop of Worcester, condemned the blacksmiths' Sunday working, but they ignored him, hammering all the louder to drown his voice. The bishop cursed them, and every one of them grew a horsetail which so embarrassed them that they shunned their customers, and the trade died out in the town.

Two factors contributed to the magical reputation of horseshoes, and their centuries-old popularity as a protective talisman over the doors of houses, or nailed in the deckhouse or to the masts of ships. Cold iron was regarded as effective against demons and evil magic. Even today amongst sailors, to say the words 'cold iron' is regarded as a protective charm if one has inadvertently risked bad luck.

In the Scottish Highlands, iron is regarded as a protection

against spiteful fairies. A hunter will plunge his knife into the body of a deer he has killed, to prevent the fairies putting their weight upon it to make it difficult for him to carry home. Also the music of a Jew's harp, because of its steel tongue, is believed to frighten off such malevolent spirits.

In Morocco, a steel knife is put under a sick person's pillow to keep evil spirits away. The Bengalese carry a piece of iron on their person for the same purpose; their wives wear a protective steel bangle, even if it is gold-plated. If a woman dies in childbirth, a nail or other small iron item is put in her funeral dress to prevent her spirit from returning and stealing the child. The Sinhalese have similar beliefs.

The Roman author Pliny maintained that 'if nails that have been taken from a tomb are driven into the threshold of a door, they will prevent nightmares'.

On the positive side, the crescent shape of the horseshoe has always been regarded as symbolizing the Moon Goddess, bestower of fertility and domestic good fortune.

The seventeenth-century writer John Aubrey observed: 'Most houses at the west-end of London have a horseshoe on the threshold.' In the next generation, the poet John Gay wrote of his domestic defences:

> Straws laid across my path retard;
> The horse-shoe's nailed, each threshold's guard.

The custom lasted well into the nineteenth century. It is recorded that in Monmouth Street off Shaftesbury Avenue, there were seventeen such door horseshoes in 1813, and still seven in 1855.

Specially powerful as protective and good-luck talismans are said to be horseshoes which have been found by accident, or which come from the near hind hoof of a grey mare.

The general method is to display the horseshoe points upwards, to prevent the luck running out. But blacksmiths and farriers have always displayed it points downwards, to pour power on to the forge, and they still universally do so. (Janet's husband's ancestors were farriers, hence the name Farrar, and all Farrars or Farrers who are entitled to a coat of arms have horseshoes which point downwards on their shields.) In past centuries, some doorway horseshoes of non-blacksmiths used to be mounted points downwards, to pour power over the door as a protective shield – and in the North of England particularly, for the additional reason that the Devil could not sit in it. The downward-pointing habit, however, seems to have become a smith's monopoly.

Lord Nelson had a horseshoe nailed to the mast of his flagship the *Victory*. There were those who said that if the horseshoe had not been pointing downwards, he would not have died at Trafalgar in 1805. So by then at least the smiths' monopoly was widely accepted.

Symbols of a tradesman's speciality, displayed outside his door, used to be general, and deriving from traditional roots. The three brass balls of the pawnbroker, for example, were the three gold spheres of the Lombardy coat of arms – representing the three bags of gold which St Nicholas brought down the chimney for three unmarried sisters who had no dowries ('Santa Claus's' first action of this kind). Lombardy goldsmiths used this symbol when they set up business abroad, and they were customarily bankers and loan merchants as well as goldsmiths. Or the barber's pole with its spiral markings, recalling the fact that when bleeding was a traditional therapy, it was barbers who performed it – the spirals representing bandages.

Most of these traditional trade symbols have died out in this century. It is still rare, however, to find even the most modern blacksmith's forge which does not have a points-down horseshoe at the door.

The horseshoe is the symbol of England's tiniest county, Rutland (which sadly no longer officially exists as an independent administrative entity). A centuries-old tradition lays down that any member of the Royal Family, or any peer of the realm, who visits Rutland must present the lord of the manor of Oakham with a horseshoe. The castle at Oakham has a collection of over 200 of these tributes, the oldest of which (dated about 1600) is said to have been given by Elizabeth I. The largest was from George IV; it cost £20 to make, and the king left the lord of the manor to pay the bill.

Not all the stories of blacksmiths' magical powers are pagan. An anvil is still kept in the Methodist church at Aberford in Yorkshire in memory of Samuel Hick, a local nineteenth-century blacksmith who prayed for wind to grind corn needed by the congregation. The wind immediately sprang up and turned the mill. As soon as the grinding was complete, the air was still again.

The extremely talented tenth-century St Dunstan, who was a musician, painter, embroiderer and metalworker as well as becoming Abbot of Glastonbury and finaly Archbishop of Canterbury, was said once to have shod the Devil himself. The Devil screamed for mercy and ran away, swearing never to go near a horseshoe again.

A similar story comes from Yarrow in Selkirkshire. Two brothers were apprenticed to a blacksmith, and the younger one became the victim of a malignant witch. She would put a magic bridle on him at night and this turned him into a horse which she rode off to her coven meetings.

When the older brother discovered what was happening, he followed them and managed to slip the bridle off the boy and on to the witch instead. She at once became a mare, whom he rode till she was exhausted and then took to the blacksmith to be shod. Next day, the witch was found writhing in agony, with a horseshoe nailed to each of her hands and feet.

A very early saint – Clement, third Bishop of Rome after St Peter – became the patron of blacksmiths because he had been martyred by drowning with an iron anchor tied to his neck. His festival, on 23 December, may well have inherited the features, as well as the date, of that of Weyland the Smith.

St Clement's Day was marked until late in the nineteenh century by blacksmiths enacting a curious legend about King Alfred trying to determine which trade was paramount. At first he named the tailor, because of the beauty of a coat he had made; but the indignant blacksmith went on strike, as a result of which all the other craftsmen, including the tailor, soon ran out of the tools for which they depended on the blacksmith.

At last, when the king's horse cast a shoe, the desperate craftsmen broke into the smithy and tried to forge one themselves. They only succeeded in knocking over the anvil, which exploded. St Clement and the blacksmith then appeared, and King Alfred finally reversed his decision and named the blacksmith as the prince of craftsmen, on whom all others depended. The furious tailor slashed the blacksmith's apron – since when smiths have always worn ragged aprons.

The ritual re-enactment involved a blacksmith robed as 'Old Clem' being escorted through the town by his colleagues, who collected beer-money from the bystanders, and finally by filling an anvil's hole with gunpowder and exploding it with a hammer blow.

Incidentally, not all blacksmiths were (or, of course, are) men. Marged vch Ifan of Llanberis in Carnarvonshire, born in 1696 was said to have been the strongest woman ever to have lived in Wales, and was a first-rate blacksmith, harp-maker, tailor and carpenter. Many legends became attached to her. When she was 70 it was said she could still out-wrestle any man in Wales, and catch ten times as many foxes as the local hunt. She married (and twice beat up) the most effeminate of her many suitors, and lived to be 105.

A horseshoe nail is involved in a strange auction at Aldermaston village hall in Berkshire every three years. The auction is for the lease rights of lands owned by the Church. The nail is stuck sideways into a candle, and once it is lit, bidding begins. When the candle burns down to the nail, the flame dies and the nail drops out. The last bid made before this happens obtains the lease, and the rent from it is devoted to charity. The candle auction was revived in 1815, but it had existed for several centuries before that.

Ripley in Surrey used to be called by its Woking neighbours

'The Place Where They Shoe Dead Horses', and when a Woking man met a Ripley man he would flap an imaginary apron at him. The story was that a Ripley blacksmith had thrown a horse down on the green to shoe it, but had failed to notice that it had died from a heart attack. He shod it, and then flapped his apron at it again and again to try to wake it.

The days when the blacksmith was the prince of craftsmen, and the keystone of manufacture, are gone. Industrial machinery, and modern technology, have relegated him to the sidelines.

Sad, perhaps, but one cannot put the clock back. Technological advance, it has to be admitted, has greatly improved ordinary people's standard of living (even if it has introduced ecological damage which is only beginning to be realistically tackled). There is a silver lining; the same technology increasingly releases men and women from routine drudgery, and points the way to their concentrating on specifically human activities which the factory-line or the computer cannot fulfil.

In the blacksmith's case, this can mean releasing him from such tasks as mere tool-making, and calling upon him to turn his efforts to artistry in metal – for example, beautiful gates where something more than a factory product is called for. In work like that, nothing can replace the individual craftsman.

He (or she) is still the only one to shoe horses, and, we suspect, always will be.

Before we leave the subject – one magical function of the metalworker, even before the discovery of iron, was the making of protective talismans for horses, whose known psychic sensitivity was believed to make them particularly vulnerable to the Evil Eye. These talismans have survived till today, in the form of horse brasses, even though their original function may have been forgotten.

Genuine original horse brasses are far rarer today, than the many reproductions turned out for the souvenir trade. But these are at least usually copied from or based on original designs, and the magical protective motifs can still be seen, such as solar, lunar and stellar symbols, oak leaves and acorns, Lady Godiva, points-down horseshoe designs, and so on.

Celtic artefacts from early times, such as those of the La Tene culture, are rich in such protective metalwork. 'Many of the elaborate horse trappings and helmet decorations can be seen to display the insignia of magical power, and evil-averting properties' (Anne Ross, *Everyday Life of the Pagan Celts*, p.197)

In the first century BC, enamelling, by the champleve technique, began to be added to the already fine artistry of such trappings – but only in Britain, where it originated among the Belgic tribes of Kent and Suffolk. Handsome examples of such work have been found as far north as Kirkcudbright in Scotland. It seems to have died out, however, as Roman occupation swamped the native culture.

Horses are not the only mount protected by such talismans. Bedouins' camels still are – and their practice must be at least four thousand years old, because the Bible records that when Gideon defeated the Midianites, he 'took the ornaments that were on their camels' necks' (Judges viii 21). Significantly, the Revised Version and the New English Bible both render 'ornaments' as 'crescents' – the symbols of the Moon Goddess.

VII *Folklore and Fairytale*

Hoofprints in stone, or in any soft surface which has hardened enough for them to be permanent, tend to have legends attached to them. For example, in a deep cut in the cliff of Aughris Head in County Sligo, there is a flagstone showing hoof marks. They are said to be those of the famous white horse of O'Dowd, ruler of the barony of Tireragh. In the same area, immediately north of Tullaghan Hill in a gap through the Ox Mountains from Lugnadiffe, there is a stone said to retain the hoofmark of St Patrick's horse.

St Patrick's horse also appears in a legend of Carrickatuke, a high peak on a ridge in County Armagh. There is said to be a Sod of Truth there, brought from the Land of Promise, which upturns if a lie is spoken on it. St Patrick's nag is said to have rested on it, and, according to one version, a single grain from the load he was carrying fell there.

W.W. Gill says in his 1929 work *A Manx Scrapbook* (quoted by Máire MacNeill in *The Festival of Lughnasa* p.355):

> 'St Patrick when crossing from Ireland on horseback was pursued by a sea-monster which must have been opposed to the conversion of the Island; to escape it the horse made a leap up the cliffside, and at the place where it landed the well gushed out. The (petrified) monster may be seen at the foot of the gully below. A similar legend pertains to St Maughold's Well, minus the monster.' The name of the landing-point is given as Chibber Pherick ('Patrick's Well' in the old Manx language).

The horse seems to have left his magic at the spot. Chibber Pherick is next to a stone called the White Lady of Ballafreer, and the well and the stone are both considered powerful in promoting the fertility of women. The woman would take a mouthful of the well water before sunrise, walk three times round the stone deosil (the way of the sun), swallow the water, and then say 'In the name of the Father, the Son, and the Holy Ghost.'

The saint's horse could carry any load. A story from near Croagh Patrick in County Mayo, Ireland's holiest mountain, tells how the workmen building a church for Patrick were short of food. Patrick took them and his horse to the well-filled barn of a man called Black Cormac, and asked what he would charge for as much meal as the horse could carry on its back. A price was agreed and paid, and the men brought out a big bag of meal. Cormac said it would break the nag's back, but Patrick ordered them to go on loading till he told them to stop. They put on bag after bag till the load was 'as big as a small house', which the horse carried away easily – to Black Cormac's understandable anger.

Possession of a horse was characteristic of a chief, king, god or goddess, and as many of the St Patrick legends can be shown to have been originally those of the brilliant Young God Lugh (who was said to have invented horsemanship), so doubtless some of the tales of his horse were once told of Lugh's. In most cultures, 'the gods of the old religion become the devils of the new', but Ireland is a notable exception to this. Irish pagan gods and goddesses became legendary heroes and heroines – or even saints, as in the case of St Brighid (Bridget), patron of poets, healers and blacksmiths. St Brighid inherited the legends, seasonal rituals, and holy places of Brighid the goddess of inspiration, healing and craftsmanship and was in many aspects quite unchanged.

The name of Lough Patrick in County Tyrone commemorates the saint's disapproval of a local pagan tradition, which said (and still says) that a horse used to rise out of the lake every seven years. Máire MacNeill (ibid. p.256) reports a local resident as saying:

A unicorn with the Scottish shield at Holyrood Palace, Edinburgh

The white horse in Westbury, Wiltshire

Centaur fighting with Lapith (Elgin Marbles, British Museum)

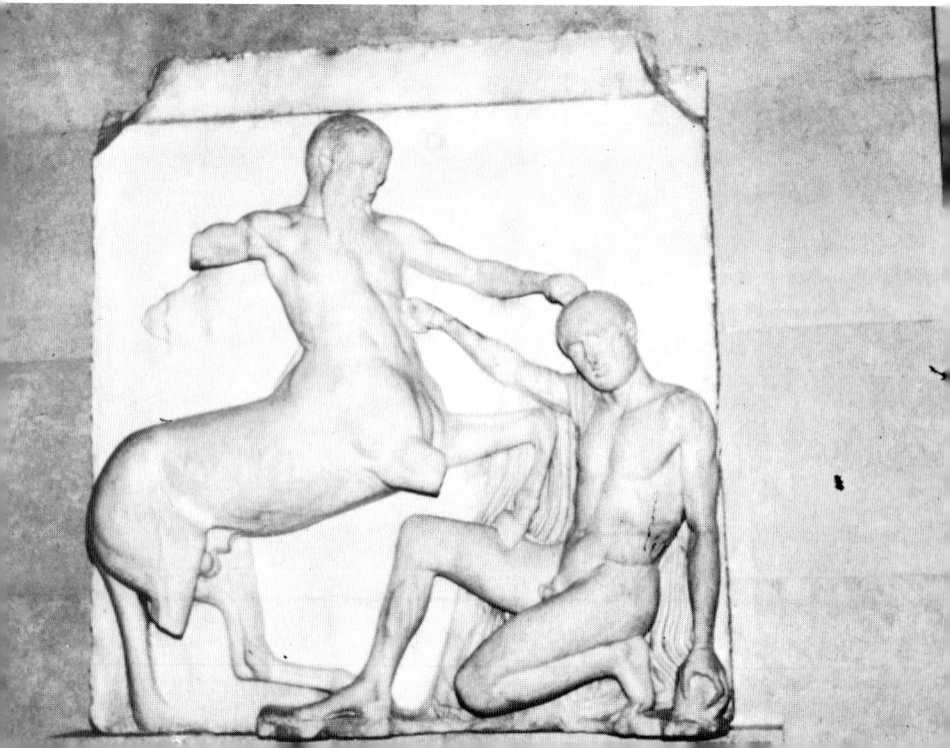

A hippocampus – in Greek mythology. The marine equivalent of a Centaur

Horse head statue at Corinth, Greece

Pegasus, the flying horse

'It has occurred to me that the lake's original name was Loch an Eich [the lake of the horse] and that it was connected with horse-worship, and that that is why Patrick turned aside there to build a church. But the pagan tradition stuck on in the name of the church – Domnach an Eich – and in the still surviving legend about the horse appearing.'

Máire MacNeill comments: 'This surmise is most probably a valid one. Preternatural horses have left many tracks in the traditions of Tyrone.'

The hamlet is called Doncaneigh, obviously a slurring of Domnach an Eich. The local priest always holds a service on 'Lough Sunday', the first Sunday in August, on which day the waters of the lake are said to cure every ailment – reminding us of the familiar healing element in horse cults.

The healing (or protection from illness) theme crops up in another St Patrick story. After Patrick had baptized the pagan Oisin, he gave Oisin a horse, but told him that if he dismounted he would lose his health. Oisin forgot the warning and dismounted to help some men lift a heavy stone, and immediately felt ill.

At Benaghlin, a hill above Lough Erne in County Fermanagh, a story appears in an old manuscript that a huge sleek silky horse used to rise up to its middle out of the peak a Samhain (Hallowe'en) and tell anyone who asked it everything that would happen to him up to the next Samhain. This was believed to have happened long in the past, because the manuscript said offerings used to be left on the peak for the horse 'until the time of St Patrick and the holy clerics', i.e. presumably till the Church clamped down on the pagan practice.

Also near Lough Erne, a height called Topped Mountain has a little lake on the side from which a water-horse is said to rise and cross the heath to Loughascaul, which it enters, it is presumed, to visit some similar creature.

An English horse with a remarkable reputation belonged to a fifteenth-century Shropshire highwayman called Wild Humphrey Kynaston. Both are said to have lived in a cavern which is still known as Kynaston's Cave, on Nesscliffe Hill near Great Ness. Kynaston was popular locally for his Robin Hood reputation of stealing from the rich to give to the poor, so neither he nor his horse ever lacked for food. Like Dick Turpin and the Young Pretender, Kynaston had the habit of shoeing his horse back-to-front to confuse pursuers, but if the abilities with which his horse is credited were true, that would seem to have been hardly necessary. It is said that it once jumped the nine miles from Nesscliffe Hill to Ellesmere with Kynaston on its back, and that on another occasion it jumped him over the River Severn at a point where it is forty feet wide, and which is still known as Kynaston's Leap.

Small wonder that some (presumably his rich victims) maintained that Kynaston had sold his soul to the devil, or even that the horse was the Devil himself. Local support, however, kept Wild Humphrey Kynaston safe to the end; he was never caught, and he finally died peacefully in his cave.

We only know of one case where the legendary 'highwayperson' was the horse alone. In Epping Forest in Essex, near where Janet grew up, there was said to have been a white mare who stopped coaches passing through the forest; the coach-horses would not budge until the travellers had handed over their valuables to the mare. She too had a Robin Hood reputation. She kept her gains in a secret 'mare's nest' near Epping Upland, and gifts from her hoard would appear during the night on the doorsteps of the needy. The mare's nest is reputed still to exist, with the remains of her treasure if only one could find it. (This is a kindlier version of the treasure-guarding mare's nest monster we mentioned previously.)

The horse of Dartmoor highwayman Tom Faggus, an historically factual character who appears in R.D. Blackmore's novel *Lorna Doone*, was so well trained that local people believed it was his familiar spirit. It was said that if his horse had not been shot first, Faggus would never have been caught to be hanged at Taunton.

Talking of Dartmoor – the champion passenger-carrying

horse of all time must be Tom Pearse's grey mare of the West Country song, who carried six men plus Old Uncle Tom Cobleigh to Widecombe Fair. Legendary she may be, but Tom Cobleigh certainly existed; he was a farmer from Spreyton in North Devon, twelve miles from Widecombe. There were several Tom Cobleighs in the family's history, but the most likely one to have been referred to in the song died in 1794 and is buried in an unmarked grave in Spreyton churchyard. (The nearby Tom Cobleigh stone is that of his nephew.) He was a notorious womanizer with bright red hair.

Widecombe Fair still takes place on the second Thursday in September, and 'Uncle Tom' always appears at it, complete with grey mare.

The madness of the people of Gotham in Nottinghamshire is remembered in the nursery rhyme:

> Three wise men of Gotham
> Went to sea in a bowl;
> And if the bowl had been stronger,
> My song would have been longer.

In fact the village's 'madness' was deliberate, to discourage King John from building a hunting lodge there, at the cost of much of their land. The ploy was successful, the villagers' ingenuity in feigning madness prompting the king to look elsewhere.

Two of their contrived acts of madness involved horses. In one, a horse had drunk from a pool in which the Moon was reflected, just as a cloud obliterated the reflection. Its owner claimed the horse had swallowed the Moon, and chopped the animal in two to get it back.

The other was less rough on the horse. Its owner had to take two bushels of wheat to Nottingham market, but to spare his beast he carried the wheat on his back, while riding the horse.

A popular belief which still survives concerns the weakness of white-footed horses. The more white feet it has, the belief maintains, the more vulnerable it is to leg injuries. In England, there are rhymes such as:

> If you have a horse with four white feet, keep him not a day;
> If you have a horse with three white feet, send him far away;
> If you have a horse with two white feet, sell him to a friend;
> If you have a horse with one white foot, keep him to the end.

Or more succinctly:

> One, buy it;
> Two, try it;
> Three, doubt it;
> Four, do without it.

An Irish equivalent recommends:

> One, buy it;
> Two, try it;
> Three, look it over;
> Four, turn it out to clover.

Most vets would write this off as superstition, but we have met owners who insist that their experience confirms it. One of them pointed out, in support of the logic of the belief, that horses with white face-markings are liable to sunburn.

Numerologists maintain that their system is helpful in backing horses. As Richard Cavendish writes (*The Black Arts*, p.68):

> According to numerologists, you can use numbers not only to assess your own character but also to improve your life and fortunes ... If you back a horse it should carry number 5 and the race should be run on a day which adds up to 5. If the jockey's name or birth date also adds up to 5, you have a sure thing.

The numerology of a name is based on this table:

1	2	3	4	5	6	7	8	9
A	B	C	D	E	F	G	H	I
J	K	L	M	N	O	P	Q	R
S	T	U	V	W	X	Y	Z	

You add up the numbers of the letters of the name. If there are two or more digits in the total, you add these up in turn, repeating the process if the new total is above 9, till you end up with a single digit, e.g. 17 becomes 8, 20 becomes 2, 129 becomes 12 and then 3, and so on. Richard Cavendish's name, for example, thus ends up as 2.

One would have thought that some statistical research into the racing records would have established whether or not this punters' principle is sound, but so far as we know that has never been done, and people keep on hopefully using it! (And Lester Piggott's name, to pick an outstanding example, adds up to 2.)

The kelpies, also known as Nykurs, were grey or black; their hooves pointed backwards, and the tufts on their pasterns were reversed. If one of them mated with an ordinary horse, the offspring would always lie down in the water when crossing a ford. A kelpie could change shape at will. One of the forms it often took was that of a Boobrie – a huge bird-shaped creature whose claw-prints were as large as a pair of antlers, and who roared like an angry bull. It haunted the freshwater and sea lochs of Argyllshire, devouring sheep and cows.

One person seems to have benefited from a confrontation with a kelpie. He was Grigor Willox, a famous eighteenth-century white witch who lived in Tomintoul, Banffshire, the highest village in Britain, but who operated all over the north of Scotland. Tradition says he did nothing but good. One of the talismans he always carried with him was a brass hook from a kelpie's bridle, which he had captured from the water-horse of Loch Ness.

Northern mythology tells of seahorses which sometimes slept on ice floes, mostly between Norway and Britain. They had horses' heads, cows' hooves, and hind parts like fishes. They hunted for food both at sea and on land.

In the north of England, the word 'dobbie' (thought to be cognate with 'Dobbin', and possibly stemming from the same root as the Gaelic *dubh*, 'black') means a kind of horse apparition, big, black and shaggy and more likely to be seen out of the corner of the eye than straight ahead. Dobbie-stones are stones with a natural hole in the centre, and are used to fend off evil, black magic, and dobbies in particular.

A lady living in the Forest of Bowland, in West Yorkshire, has a dobbie-stone hanging by her front door. She told Guy Ragland-Phillips (*Brigantia: A Mysteriography*, p.189): 'I have three sisters, and each of us has one of these hanging by the door. Gypsies never call on any of us. They see that stone from the gate and go by.'

Dobbie-stones are mainly, and widely, found in the North, but one bloodstock horse-breeder in Sussex keeps one, hanging by the stable door, and calls it by that name. If one of his mares has a black foal, he calls it a dobbie.

The herb fennel is said to have a magical effect on animals; snakes are said to eat it to help them shed their skins. Also, a straying horse, it is claimed, can be brought to order by offering it fennel-flavoured gingerbread. (There may be an element of truth in this belief; the smell of fennel is not unlike that of aniseed, which many mammals are known to find difficult to resist.)

The behaviour of horses at a funeral, in the days when hearses were horse-drawn, was regarded as particularly significant. If they refused to start with the coffin, it meant that someone else in the family would soon die, and if a funeral horse on its way to the graveyard turned its head towards a house and neighed, somebody in that house was also nearing his or her end.

A way of gaining power over horses was by becoming a

'toadman'. This meant pinning a toad over an anthill until the ants had stripped its skeleton bare. You then took the skeleton and threw it into a swiftly flowing stream. If one of the bones detached itself and started moving against the current, screaming as it went, you had to capture it. This bone would then give you complete dominance over horses.

An extension of this said that having obtained the precious bone, you had to take it for three consecutive nights to a graveyard or a stable. On the third night, the Devil would appear, and try to get the bone from you. Only if you managed to keep possession of it would you become a fully fledged toadman. It is suggested that this is the origin of the surname Todman.

A strange legend among foxhunters is that foxes will run to the grave, or the home, of a hunter soon after his death. There was an instance of this in Gloucestershire which was reported in *Horse and Hound* for 3 January 1991. The journal commented that 'it has occurred on many occasions, but none was more remarkable'.

The Duke of Beaufort's hounds had been due to meet on 22 December 1990. Major Gerald Gundry, a member of the hunt, had died two days previously, but he had expressed a wish that hunting should not be cancelled on his account. So the hunt met at Foxley Green as arranged, observed a minute's silence in the Major's honour, and set off.

There was a shortage of foxes, and little scent, but at about 2.30, a fox bolted of its own accord, and hounds pursued it. It gained a 1½ minutes' lead, but they finally caught up with it in the garden of Major Gundry's house, Clayfields, about five yards from the front door.

Capt. Ian Farquhar, Joint Master and huntsman, wrote to *Horse and Hound*: 'In living memory no one could remember a fox being caught in the Clayfields gardens. No further fox was found on that day. All those present, myself included, could not but feel that they had witnessed something rather special.'

It hardly needs pointing out that the horse plays a great part in fairy-tales. The milk-white steed of the knight in shining armour, or of the prince who comes to awaken the sleeping beauty, seems an essential part of his personality – the horse itself symbolizing his virility and determination, and its colour the purity of his purpose. (The fact that it is always 'milk-white', and never simply described in customary jargon as 'grey', emphasizes that the description is symbolic rather than technical.) The magical horses of the Arabian Nights have similar symbolism.

The same rule seems to apply to history which has become legend, as well as to simple fairy-tale. It is very unlikely, for example, that Joan of Arc rode anything but an ordinary cavalry or even farm horse into battle, of one of the various shades of brown; or that she wore anything over her simple peasant dress other than protective leather or perhaps chain-mail. Romantic pictures of her, however, always clothe her in a sort of brassiered breastplate, symbolizing the female assuming a male warrior role without losing her essential femininity – and her steed is, it goes without saying, milk-white, as befits a heroic virgin saint. (One wonders if some artists have not been tempted to make it a unicorn, but have resisted the temptation so that they could still persuade themselves and others that they were portraying history!)

One of the richest sources of fairy-tales is *The Thousand and One Nights*, usually referred to as *The Arabian Nights* (see Bibliography under Mathers) – the nightly stories which Scheherazade told her King. This collection is liberally sprinkled with magical horses.

For example, The Tale of Pomegranate-Flower and Badr Basim tells of a wicked Queen Almanakh who was a powerful sorceress. It was her habit to seduce young men, make them mate with her incessantly till they were exhausted, and then to turn them into horses or asses – continuing to mate with them at will by taking the form of a mare. The young prince Badr Basim managed to circumvent her magic and defeat her, restore her countless victims to human shape and, of course, find himself the princess of his own choice.

In another, The Magic Tale of the Ebony Horse, a cunning sage creates a horse which can be made to fly in the air, covering in a day the distance which would take a normal horse a year. He brings it to the King, who promises him the hand of one of his beautiful daughters. The princess is horrified, however, as the man is old and ugly. So the princess's brother takes a hand, gets control of the horse, experiences many marvellous advenures on it, and ends up by saving his sister from a fate worse than death and bringing home a lovely princess for himself. The creator of the horse, who had lied and cheated in an attempt to eliminate the prince, was executed on the King's orders.

In The Master of the White Mare, the hero is turned into a dog by a girl 'from the Isles of the Far North' whom he had intended to be his bride, but who proves to be an evil sorceress. He is finally restored to human form by another girl who recognizes what he truly is, and who provides him with a spell by which he turns the sorceress into a white mare. 'Since then,' Scheherazade reports him as saying, 'I have been lawfully married to the girl who saved me, and have exorcized the devil in that wicked woman every day upon the polo ground.'

VIII *Festival Horses*

Horses have played an important part in the seasonal rituals and festivals in many European cultures, but nowhere more so than in Ireland. In many places there, the traces still linger.

Most widespread of these communal festival assemblies were at Lughnasa (Festival of Lugh), at the end of July and the beginning of August. Lughnasa is the Gaelic name for the month of August and it is called after Lugh, a mythological hero who was originally in fact the brilliant Young God who, in many pantheons, succeeds (by defeating or slaying) the simpler, and in some ways cruder, Old God of earlier days. He symbolizes the greater sophistication and technological advance of the culture concerned, for the expression of which new archetypes were needed. Lugh's filling of this role is revealed in his titles of Lugh Samhioldanach (Of Many Arts) and Lugh Lamhfhada (Of the Long Arm), and the Old God he overcame was Balor, his grandfather, who failed first to prevent his daughter Eithne bearing him, and then to kill him as a child. Lugh also gave his name to County Louth (Lughbhaidh).

Ireland's pagan deities were transformed into the heroes and heroines of mythological prehistory, and have so remained in folklore and legend and the stories told of Lugh adhere to this pattern.

The most important of the Lughnasa festival gatherings, which lasted in one form or another from pre-Christian times into the nineteenth century was Oenach Tailten, at Tailtiu (now called Teltown) on the northern bank of the river Blackwater in

County Meath, halfway between today's Navan and Kells. Its importance stemmed from the fact that it was presided over by the high king of Ireland. Meath (in Gaelic, *Midhe*, 'middle') was the high king's territory, separate from the four provinces of Ulster, Leinster, Connacht and Munster, in the same way and for the same reason as the District of Columbia is distinct from all the States of the USA, or Canberra from those of Australia.

The actual origins of Oenach Tailten are lost in prehistory, though legend says that Tailtiu was the name of Lugh's foster-mother (another goddess-turned-heroine), who died on 1 August, from exhaustion at having single-handedly uprooted the trees of the forest (which occupied the area of Meath), to transform it into rich farmland. Lugh founded Oenach Tailten in her honour, and it must be significant that the traditional creator of that farmland (among the best in Ireland) was honoured at what was in effect a harvest festival.

Christianity recognized Oenach Tailten from the start, St Patrick himself blessing the site. As a royal occasion, it continued till the Norman takeover of Ireland in the twelfth century. Thereafter it survived as a peasant festival till about 1770, and for a generation or two after that on the other bank of the Blackwater.

It may seem excessive to explain Oenach Tailten in such detail in a book about horse magic. So it would be, if the horse-racing which was a feature of it had been merely sport. Even apart from the fact, however, that Lugh was said to have invented horse-racing, and indeed horsemanship itself, there are clear indications that it had a ritual significance of central importance to the Oenach.

One story in particular underlines this. High King Daire was presiding at the festival, and it had been prophesied that a son of his called Lugaid would succeed him. He had six sons of that name, however, so he asked a druid which of them would become High King after him. The six were horse-racing at the time, and the druid told him it would be the one who could catch a fawn which had appeared in the assemby. The sons rode off chasing it, far into Leinster, and it was finally caught by the son called Lugaid Laige.

They then sought lodging, one by one, at the only house in sight, which was owned by a hideous old hag. She would only grant it to the one who would mate with her. Only Lugaid Laige was brave enough; and as soon as he did so, she turned into a beautiful woman, who told him she was the Sovereignty of Ireland. In the morning, house and woman had vanished, and the six rode back to Tailtiu and told the King and his company what had happened. Thereupon the assembly dispersed.

The Goddess of Sovereignty, with whom the heir must have intercourse before his title is validated, is a recurring theme in all pagan traditions, and nowhere has evidence of this concept survived more clearly than in Ireland. In a sense she represents the land itself, whose fruitfulness depends on the king's intimate binding to her, and he must prove his worthiness before she will accept him.

So this story sums up the ritual process: the horse symbolizing the contest for title, and the Goddess the validation. All that achieved, and proclaimed to the assembly, the purpose of that particular festival is over, and the men of Ireland can return to their homes.

Another incident is worth mentioning – a historically recorded one, this time. In 811 the High King Aed Oirdnidhe tried to hold the Oenach as usual, but the religious community of Tallaght placed a ban on it, because of a breach of their sanctuary by members of the royal family, the Ui Neills. The ban was effective, and 'neither horse nor chariot' attended. The High King had to succumb, and make reparations to Tallaght. The point is clear – no horses, no Oenach.

Racing was not the only ritual involving horses at Tailtiu. Henry Morris, in the *Journal of the Royal Society of Antiquaries of Ireland* (1930) wrote:

> A custom with a distinct pagan touch was the swimming of horses in the river Blackwater before sunrise in the morning as a protection against disease. The horse carrying an almost naked rider was

jumped or plunged into a deep pool in the river; it was necessary that the horse be completely wetted by the water. This custom survived until the present generation.

This swimming of horses (and of cattle) was a ubiquitous practice. As Sir Henry Piers wrote in 1682, in his *Description of Westmeath*:

> This they observe as inviolable as if it were a point of religion, for they think no beast will live the whole year thro' unless they be thus drenched ... But precisely to do this on the first Sunday in harvest, I look on as not only superstitious, but profane.

At Lough Ouel near Mullingar, in County Westmeath, the horse-swimming was a major feature of the festival of 'Lough Sunday', the first Sunday in August, which thousands attended, at least up to the early nineteenth century. Máire MacNeill (*The Festival of Lughnasa*, pp.245–8), quotes in full a dramatic account of this event from the *Dublin Penny Journal* in 1835, involving precognitive dreams and the death of one of the young riders.

Similar accounts come from Cloonoran and Lough Nalarsach in County Galway, several sites in County Meath, Lough Ciarain in County Mayo, and many other localities.

That the horse-swimming was regarded as magical is underlined by the report of a Mr O'Conor of the Ordnance Survey in 1838, concerning the Lough Ciarain event:

> The people, it is said, swim their horses in the lake on that day, to defend them against incidental evils during the year, and throw spancers and halters into it, which they leave there on the occasion. They are also accustomed to throw butter into it, with the intention that their cows may be sufficiently productive of milk and butter during the year.

The Church had no doubt of the pagan significance of the festival, for O'Conor records:

> The priests have dissuaded the people from getting on with their ceremonies at the lake, so far that they are altogether giving them up.

On the Lughnasa festivals as a whole, Máire MacNeill writes (ibid. p.427): 'We have found the survival of Lughnasa at a hundred and ninety-five sites in Ireland. Some of these we know of only through the chance observations of earlier times. There must have been many more assemblies of which no record exists.'

There is one place within walking distance of old Tailtiu where a Lughnasa gathering still occurs – St Kieran's Well at Castlekeeran, County Meath, about three miles west of Kells. Within living memory it still involved, not the swimming for the pool is too small, but at least the splashing of horses.

A spring rises from a hillock, and sinks three times below ground before it flows into the River Blackwater. There are three old stone crosses at the site, and the base of a fourth is visible in the river. The festival is held on the first Sunday in August, and is presided over by the parish priest. The water of the little stream is believed to have special powers from midnight to midnight on that day: the various pools are reputed to cure toothache and headache, and bathing the feet at one point is said to protect them from soreness for the coming year. Until very recently, horses were still ridden through the stream in order to give them a year of protection from danger.

Up until the turn of the century, there was horse-racing in Kells itelf on the day of, and associated with, the Castlekeeran Festival.

We attended the festival ourselves on Sunday 5 August 1990. The lane was packed with cars, the usual itinerant salesmen were catering to the large crowd, and there was a general holiday atmosphere. Although we saw no horses being stream-ridden, there was no doubt that at the heart of the event, round the stream itself, a sense of the ritual importance of the occasion was as alive as ever.

Castlekeeran is only a few miles from Teltown, and there is evidence that Lugh was its patron before St Kieran took over; it may have been a sort of satellite of the Oenach Tailten. Kieran himself (c.512–545) was abbot of a monastery at Clonmacnoise,

County Meath, and had a reputation for his affinity with animals. Legend says, for example, that as a young monk he had a fox which used to carry his scripts to his master, until it became old enough to eat the satchel, when he had to give up the practice.

Another Lughnasa event which we attended in 1990 was the horse fair at the Rock of Muff in County Cavan, known as the Patron Fair. It is now a lively trading event, but its roots are much older, connected with a lake which dried up in the nineteenth century, and with a well which still survives. The water of both was held to be holy, and to have healing properties. The old festival used to last a week, and include music, dancing, horse-racing and ass-racing. An old harvest-men's song declares:

> First the Fair of Muff, and then the holiday;
> We'll meet him on the road, and well he knows the way.

The Rock of Muff would not appear to be an ideal place for a horse fair, there being no village nearby. The tradition is so strong, however, that an attempt by the shopkeepers of Kingscourt, the nearest market town, to get it moved to there some years ago failed.

An old man at the fair told us it had been held in its present form for about forty years, and that 'it's not what it used to be, when there were fiddlers on the road and all'. To his understanding, the old festival had existed for at least four hundred years before that. He told us it used to be connected with the O'Reilly castle which stood nearby, and which was said to have been demolished by Cromwell.

But as Máire MacNeill remarks with regard to the Muff castle: 'Irish popular tradition attributes the destruction of most castles to Cromwell and, while in the largest sense there is truth in the fable, occasionally and at certain sites one wonders whether Cromwell has not been superimposed on Crom Dubh.' (*The Festival of Lughnasa*, p.306) Crom Dubh was an old pagan god with whom St Patrick was said to have contended, so if

Máire MacNeill is right in this case – in other words, if the castle disappeared long before Cromwell – it may be that 440 years is a considerable underestimation of the age of the Muff festival.

IX *Horses and Witches*

The expression 'hag-ridden' stems from the belief that if a horse was found sweating and exhausted in its stable in the morning, with a tangled mane, this was because it had been conjured out by a witch during the night, ridden through the sky on her dark and mysterious journeys, and returned to its stall before dawn had awakened its owner. A protection against this possibility in Herefordshire was to prop a birch tree decorated with white and red rags against the stable door on May Day.

A round-the-year protection was to thread a holey-stone (a pebble with a natural hole right through it) and to hang it at the stable door. Holey-stones were also known as 'hag-stones' for this reason. One of these stable-protecting holey-stones in the shape of a pentacle was found a few years ago in Epping Forest.

Among the Amish communities in the United States, the 'hag-riding' explanation of overnight sweating is accepted, but they also have an alternative one. They believe that the horse has been attacked by vampires (especially if there are traces of blood).

The traditional witches' cry to make a horse gallop at incredible speeds was 'Horse and Hattock, Ho, Ho, Ho!' – a cry which was said to be used by fairies as well, for the same purpose.

Witches were also blamed for horses' unquestioned psychic sensitivity (see Chapter X). If a horse shied at something invisible to humans, or refused to pass a certain spot, it was believed to be because a witch had cast a spell on them.

Losing your temper with someone could get you the reputation of being a witch, if bad luck hit him afterwards. A Cornish example given by the nineteenth-century writer Mrs Bonham tells of a woman in the Lizard district who cursed a farmer because he reproved her for leaving a gate open and allowing his mare to stray. She told him that none of the mare's colts would ever be reared. She turned out to be right. The first was killed falling over a hedge; the second drowned in a brook; the third was kept in a stable, but slipped in a puddle and died because it was too weak to stand up; and the fourth had a malformed mouth and died of starvation. The mare had no more. Probably pure coincidence, but the woman was doubtless branded as a witch in local opinion thereafter.

Belief in witches' power over horses dies hard. Around the turn of the century, Anne Blackmore of Withypool in Somerset was said to be able to charm the horse of anyone passing her house who annoyed her. When she did, the horse would plunge and buck and sweat until Anne chose to release it.

Priss Morris, who lived in Cleobury North in Shropshire in the middle of the nineteenth century, was credited with similar powers. In her case, a horse would stop at her command, and nothing the rider or driver could do would make it move until she gave permission. Similar stories are told of the famous nineteenth-century witch of County Clare, Biddy Early. Even the local priest, who came to reprimand her, could not get his horse to move till she gave it the word.

Witches were said to be able to turn a human being into a horse by throwing a magic halter over the person's head, and then riding him or her to the sabbat. If the victim found a chance to slip off the halter, however, and throw it over the witch's head, she would be transformed into a mare, while her victim would resume human shape, and could ride her till she collapsed exhausted.

Then, of course, during the evil days of the Persecution from about the fifteenth to the seventeenth centuries, when anything up to ten million alleged witches – men, women and small children – were hanged or burned throughout Europe, any ailment of domestic animals (as well as of humans) was conveniently blamed on witchcraft. This was unfair on the genuine witches, who were often more capable healers (both human and veterinary) than the official leeches who called themselves doctors. They were, for example, much better informed herbalists, and their knowledge of psychic healing was uncluttered by official religious dogma. Most of today's genuine practitioners of 'alternative medicine', from acupuncturists to colour-therapists – and even conventional psychiatrists – would in those days doubtless have been condemned for witchcraft.

(A word here to Ireland's credit. During those terrible centuries, the fatal victims of the witch persecution in Ireland could be numbered on two hands.)

The late fifteenth-century work *Malleus Maleficarum* (Hammer of the Witches), written by the Dominicans Heinrich Kramer and James Sprenger, with the direct blessing of Pope Innocent VIII, founder of the notorious Inquisition, became the textbook of the witch persecution. This terrible book accepted wholeheartedly every wild belief about witches, gave detailed instructions for the torture of suspects to extract confessions, and so on. It probably did more to launch and shape the murderous campaign of the following couple of centuries than any other single factor.

In its lengthy and pseudo-learned exposition, it explains among other many things the 'three deceptions' by which witches could turn humans into horses and other beasts of burden (p.272 of the Arrow Books 1971 edition):

> First, that those men were caused by a glamour to seem to be changed into beasts of burden, and this change was caused in the way we have said. Second, that devils invisibly bore those burdens up when they were too heavy to be carried. Third, that those who seemed to others to be changed into beasts; as it happened to Nabuchodonosor, who lived for seven years eating straw like an ox.

Elsewhere (pp.316–17) they quote the alleged confessions of a pair of witches accused of killing twenty-three horses by evil spellworking, which were that they had initiated the spell, but that the devil had completed it. The authors add:

> From this it is concluded that the witch co-operates sufficiently if it is only by a touch or a look; for the devil is permitted no power of injuring creatures without some co-operation on the part of the witch ... and this is for the great offence to the Divine Majesty.

The persecutors, and the Church, obviously claimed a monopoly of counteraction against such deeds. The authors devote a whole chapter (pp.398–405) to warnings against using folk spells such as 'superstitious words or actions', including the reciting of charms – even against those who 'do not sprinkle Holy Water over bewitched cattle, but pour it into their mouths'.

The official persecutors firmly believed in the Devil, and equally firmly believed that witches served him – and indeed that he attended coven meetings in person, often in the form of a horse, bull, stag or goat. Having these unshakeable preconceptions, they would torture suspected witches till they confessed. ('Suspected witches' is of course a euphemism; to be suspected, or to have a finger pointed at one by an enemy, was in general enough to ensure conviction.)

One American who was said to have sold his soul to the Devil was Tom Walker, born in Massachusetts in 1727. He was a poor man who suddenly and mysteriously became rich, and set up a counting-house in Boston, becoming even richer. The story goes that when he foreclosed on a luckless mortgage-holder, the Devil sent a black man on a black horse to collect him, and Walker was never seen again. His house was searched, but all his coffers were found empty, and that night the house burned down.

A more gruesome story of the Devil using a horse to claim his price is told of the Witch of Berkeley, by the chronicler William of Malmesbury. She was said to have lived about the time of the Norman Conquest, and to have been rich and well liked. But when her luck began to change, she confessed to her two most pious children, a monk and a nun, that she had become rich by selling her soul to the Devil. She begged them, when she died, to bind her coffin with three chains, and to sing psalms over it for forty days and forty nights.

On her death, they obeyed her wishes, but on the first and second nights a crowd of demons came and snapped the first two chains. The third chain proved too strong for them, so on the third night the Devil himself appeared, smashed the chain and the coffin, and dragged the woman (who had come back to life) out into the churchyard. Waiting there was a huge black horse with spikes sticking out of its body. The Devil flung her on to its back with such force that she was impaled, and the horse rode off with her and vanished. It was said that her screams could be heard from miles away.

Going back to the witch trials – the reports were written by the persecutors themselves, and even the wording of the extracted 'confessions' was often altered to suit the preconceptions we have mentioned. For example, it may well be that genuine witches under questioning sometimes referred to their God, and this would always be written down as Devil or Satan. (References to the Goddess would be ignored, because she could not be so simply equated with Satan. Shakepeare, interestingly, had no such inhibitions – his witches in *Macbeth* worshipped the goddess Hecate.)

This editing of trial reports makes it difficult to know just what factual truths lay behind them. There is no doubt, however, that coven rituals (the intent of which would be fertility of humans, livestock and crops) often did include a man dressed as an animal, to represent potent masculinity – and a stallion disguise, with a prominently enlarged phallus, would have been very suitable for this purpose. The rituals involved would have had all the natural unprudishness of pagan countryfolk, which would have provided perfect material for the inquisitors.

The leader of the coven would often appear disguised as, or riding, the coven's totem animal – there are many trial references to the Devil attending coven meetings 'riding a Great

Horse'. As Pennethorne Hughes remarks (*Witchcraft*, p.113): 'Seeing that he was probably of a better social status than the rest of the worshippers, this is not particularly remarkable.'

In a Basque witch trial at Vizcaya in 1555–6, the testimony of an eight-year-old girl, Catalina de Guesala, and of other minors was accepted against a family accused of witchcraft. Part of that evidence accused them of worshipping the Devil in the form of a jet black horse with horns and seated on a chair. Evidently, again, the coven leader was disguised as the totem animal. Fortunately for the group, they were appearing before a civil judge who merely condemned them to ducking and flogging.

Perhaps some of the horses regarded as being 'possessed', or used as disguises, by witches were simply their allies, for the psychic sensitivity of horses has been regarded by many people as magical. We previously gave examples from both Virginia's and Janet's experience of such sensitivity. Here is another.

When we shared a house in County Mayo, in the wild far West of Ireland, we had half a dozen ponies pastured on our eighteen acres of bog (this word in Ireland of course meaning peat-bed, not marsh or swamp). Rising out of the centre of this acreage was a grassy hillock, on the peak of which was a fallen megalith which must have weighed at least a dozen tons. To suit our own practices, we used this great stone as an altar, on the edge of a Circle of twenty or thirty yards in diameter facing southwards down the slope. Candles in jars marked the four cardinal points when the Circle was formally 'cast'.

When the Circle had not been cast, and the candles were absent, the ponies would graze across it normally as they did everywhere else. Time and again, however, when we were using the Circle ritually, the ponies would appear and canter round outside it – deosil (clockwise) as our custom required. On such occasions they would never enter the Circle, unless one of us rode one of them into it as part of the ritual, in which case it would come in without hesitation, and leave by the way it had entered when we dismounted and released it.

All this they apparently did quite instinctively, because we had in no way trained them to it. The effect of their silent collaboration certainly enhanced the magical atmosphere of the ritual – and impressed one of our country-wise neighbours who saw it.

An important tool of occultists, clairvoyants and witches has of course always been the Tarot pack of cards, and in recent years it has become publicly known and can be bought in many bookshops. Dozens of versions of it exist, the best known probably being the Waite pack (also known as the Ryder pack), designed by Pamela Colman Smith at the beginning of this century.

The Tarot consists of seventy-eight cards. Of these fifty-six (known as the Minor Arcana) are the basis from which the ordinary pack of playing cards evolved. They too are divided into four suits: Cups (corresponding to the ordinary Hearts), Wands (Clubs), Swords (Spades), and Pentacles (Diamonds). Each suit comprises the usual Ace to Ten, with the court cards King, Queen, and Knight (Jack), plus a Page.

The other twenty-two cards are known as the Major Arcana or Trumps. Under names such as Strength, the Lovers, the Emperor, the High Priestess, Judgement, and the Sun, they symbolize various archetypal aspects of the individual's development. (The only one of the Major Arcana which has survived into the ordinary pack is the Fool, who has become the Joker.)

It is hardly surprising that horse symbolism features in almost all Tarot packs. Perhaps one of the most significant is the Chariot, one of the Major Arcana. It shows a chariot and driver being drawn by two yoked horses (or in some packs, sphinxes), one black and the other white. The Chariot card symbolizes the balanced control of forces; the driver is handling contrasting energies, harmonizing them, and using the result to take him where he needs to go.

Two other Major Arcana feature horses – Death and the Sun. The Death card is frequently misunderstood. In fact it symbolizes the death of the outworn, and its rebirth in a more fruitful form. This tallies entirely with the horse's funerary symbolism throughout the ages. So, appropriately, the apparently grim figure of Death is riding a horse in most packs.

The Sun, on the other hand, cannot be misunderstood; it represents fulfilment, achievement – the integration of all the preceding Major Arcana. So in many packs (including the Waite) the blazing Sun shines on the individual, represented by a joyous child, innocence restored, riding a white horse which symbolizes the unified qualities and energies which are now understood and at the individual's disposal.

Among the Minor Arcana, all four Knights are normally mounted. The Knight of Wands represents energetic movement and activity (not in a warlike sense though). The Knight of Cups is quieter, representing creative imagination. The Knight of Swords, as one might expect, symbolizes bravery and vigorous action against evil. The Knight of Pentacles' horse is large and heavy standing for endurance, responsibility, and serviceability.

One other card of the Minor Arcana shows a mounted rider – the Six of Wands. The rider wears a laurel wreath, and symbolizes victory and success, or the bearing of great news.

Few systems of symbolism (and the Tarot is one of the richest) can manage without the horse.

X *Healing, Divining and Whispering*

Horse hairs, in popular tradition, have healing properties. Worn round the neck, they are said to cure goitre. To eradicate worms from children, horse hairs were put into their sandwiches. (They could apparently provide food, too – when left in water, it used to be said they would turn into eels.)

Horse spurs, the protuberant calluses on the inside of a horse's leg, could according to John Wesley (an enthusiastic student of folk remedies) be used to cure cancer by drying and powdering them and then steeping them in warm milk and ale.

A piebald horse in particular is credited with healing powers. Not only the application of its hairs, but even the smell of its stable, is often believed to cure many different diseases. These powers extend even to its owner or rider – his or her advice on treatment of an ailment is said to be completely reliable.

In the West of Ireland, a traditional cure for whooping cough used to be to go out in the morning and walk the roads until you met a man riding a white horse. You would stop him and ask him the best cure for whooping cough. No matter how surprised or disbelieving he was, and however ludicrous the answer he gave, whatever he told you would be the right cure for you. If his suggested cure was too difficult to carry out, no harm was done; you simply ignored it, and went out again next morning to look for another man on a white horse.

(Parts of a horse could also, it seems, be used for malicious magic. An old grimoire called *The Sword of Moses* says: 'If you wish to kill a man, take mud from the two sides of the river and form it into the shape of a figure, and write upon it the name of the person, and take seven branches from seven strong palms, and make a bow from a reed with the string of horse-sinew, and place the image in a hollow, and stretch the bow and shoot with it – and may NN be destroyed.')

Closely allied to the power of healing are those of clairvoyance and divination, and horses have always been credited with them.

They are believed to be able to see evil spirits and malign entities which men and women cannot, and to warn their human partners of their presence. They are also said to refuse to approach haunted places.

We must admit we have apparent evidence of this ourselves. When Virginia and her mother lived in County Waterford, their house was a few hundred yards from the ruins of a small village wiped out by plague, and by the great Potato Famine of 1845–7. Little remained to be seen but the outlines of the houses' foundations, but the place was said to be haunted and even sceptics agreed it had a gloomy atmosphere.

A small lane led up to the site – and where this lane entered what used to be the village, Virginia's normally disciplined ponies would come to a halt and be most reluctant to go further. She tried to pasture one of them overnight in an available field just beyond this point, but he jumped two hedges higher than he would usually have attempted, and hurried home.

Itinerants (among the most active of Ireland's horse-traders) often parked their motor-caravans in the area, and turned their horses loose to graze 'the long acre' – the grass of the lane verge. We noticed, however, that their hoofprints always stopped at the same point in the lane where Virginia's ponies baulked.

Janet's family also has a story of such horse sensitivity. Her great-grandfather, an East Anglian farmer, bought a new horse, Owd Bob, and rode him home one night during a thunderstorm. Owd Bob however, flatly refused to go over a hill on the normal route. His owner had to ride a longer way round, and arrived at his farm furious, soaking wet, and swearing to sell the 'stupid' horse.

A neighbour who had lived all his life in the district, however, told him: 'You'll be a fool if you do. That hill is full of iron, and lightning always makes for it in a storm. People have been killed. That horse's got more sense than you have. Hang on to him.'

Janet's great-grandfather prudently did so.

Sometimes, apparently a human may also see the entity which is scaring a horse. Dermot Mac Manus, a friend of W.B. Yeats, tells how when his father was a boy of about fourteen, he was in the loft above the family stable when he heard the two horses in the stall below plunging and snorting frantically. He looked down through the trapdoor, and saw about twelve feet away the thing that was terrifying the horses – 'a figure of evil with baleful eyes, blazing red like glowing coals of fire … The fingers were bone and sinew and ended not in human nails but in curved, pointed claws.' He slammed the trapdoor shut, fled to the house, and never forgot the experience for the rest of his life. (Mac Manus, *The Middle Kingdom*, pp.135–8)

At one time Janet worked in the same office as a woman from Transylvania, classic home of belief in vampires. This woman told her that horses' sensitivity used to be used there to track down graves in which undetected vampires hid during daylight. A pre-pubescent virgin child, boy or girl, would be mounted on a white horse, and the horse taken to the graveyard. It would be led from grave to grave, stepping over each – and when it came to a grave it refused to step over, that was taken to contain a vampire, and the traditional method of a wooden stake through the heart would be used to despatch it.

Virginia has heard the same story from another source, but without mention of a child rider. Hungarians, too, believe a way to identify a vampire's grave is to take a white stallion, who has never stumbled and never been to stud, into the graveyard and lead him over the various graves. (In this case, it is the horse who must be virgin.) He will refuse to walk over one belonging to a vampire.

Using horses for divination was known as hippomancy. The Celts used to walk sacred horses in procession behind a chariot, and read the future from their movements.. In pagan Germany, horses were watched coming out of temples; if they emerged right foot first, the omen was favourable; left foot first implied a warning.

Belief in the omen value of horses still survives, though local variants are sometimes contradictory. In some places it is considered lucky to encouner a white horse, while in others it means the opposite. One way of making the most of the good luck is to spit on seeing a white or piebald horse, make a wish, and keep your fingers crossed till you see a dog.

Very similar to horses' clairvoyant powers, at least in popular thinking, is the apparent ability of some of them to make mathematical calculations and even to spell out words.

Most famous of these were the Elberfeld Horses, at the turn of the century. Wilhelm von Osten of Elberfeld, Germany, trained some of his horses to do simple calculations and to tap out the answers on the floor with their hooves. Most successful was a stallion called Hans, whose name von Osten expanded to Kluge Hans (Clever Hans).

Clever Hans could not only do sums, he also learned to spell, and would indicate letters by tapping their number in the order of the alphabet. He even surprised von Osten by doing things he had not been taught. When his master wrote '35 + 12' on the blackboard, Hans tapped out the solution without being asked.

Clever Hans's fame spread, and when the Kaiser heard of him, he appointed a special commission of doctors, zoologists, trainers and other experts to investigate. They concluded that von Osten must be signalling to the horse in some unobtrusive way, but could not find out how.

In 1904, von Osten took on a partner – the wealthy jeweller Karl Krull – who carried on the work after his friend's death. Krull trained two other horses – Muhamed and Zarif – by von Osten's methods. They learned incredibly fast, and they and clever Hans became widely known as the Elberfeld Horses.

Krull speeded up the spelling process by using a chart of forty-nine squares, containing the letters (including the accented ones) of the German alphabet. The horses would indicate letters by tapping the appropriate squares, instead of having to tap out long numbers.

Muhamed in particular seems to have excelled at mathematics, coming up for example with the square roots of six-figure numbers, or with the product of two square roots.

The original commission's assumption that the required answers were being signalled by the horses' master had become very difficult to maintain. The famous Swiss psychologist Clarparade observed Krull and his horses over a long period, and wrote a report in which he excluded altogether the possibility of fraud, having become completely convinced of Krull's impeccable honesty.

Another outstanding person who studied the Elberfeld Horses closely was the 1911 Nobel Peace Prize winner and author, Maurice Maeterlink. He reported: 'The miracle comes as a surprise, the moment we set foot in it, a sort of instinctive aberration seizes us, refusing to accept the evidence and compelling us to search in every direction to see if there is not another outlet.'

Maeterlink's own summing up: 'There is probably in the horse, and probably in all that lives on earth, a psychic power similar to that which is hidden beneath the well of our reason.'

To this day no one has been able to find 'another outlet'. The astonishing achievements of the Elberfeld Horses remain unexplained by any so-called 'rational' means.

Another mathematical horse who attracted much attention in the late 1920s was Lady, a filly owned by Mrs Claudia Fonda of Richmond, Virginia. Lady also appeared to manifest extraordinary telepathic powers. Mrs Fonda had discovered this when she found she could summon Lady by simply thinking about her – and successfully repeated the method many times to rule out coincidence.

Lady attracted the interest of Dr and Mrs Rhine of Duke University, later famous for their telepathy research with human subjects using Zener cards. The Rhines had a good reputation for foolproofing such experiments, ruling out all possibility of signalling (whether deliberate or involuntary), and their investigation of Lady's gift for spelling out answers convinced them that the filly had some kind of extra-sensory perception.

Perhaps Lady's greatest achievement was when she helped the district attorney of Norfolk County, Massachusetts, in a murder hunt. A boy had been missing from his home for months, and Lady spelled out a close approximation to the name of an abandoned quarry – where the boy's body was found.

The cases of the Elberfeld Horses, Lady and other psychically gifted horses are examined in fascinating detail in Chapter 8 of Dennis Barden's book *Psychic Animals*. Particularly interesting is his account of the work of Welsh researcher Henry Blake of the Llanybyther Horse Centre in Carmarthenshire, and his technique of 'gentling' horses. This is breaking and training them by taking advantage of 'mental radio', culminating in the stage where he could direct them by merely thinking a picture of the desired route. Blake first discovered the possibility of direction by telepathy when he was training a horse called Weeping Roger.

Around Huntly in Aberdeenshire there existed for centuries a cult called the Society of the Horseman's Word. It was still very active towards the end of the nineteenth century, continuing strong until just before World War Two, and traces of it may survive to this day.

In its initiation ceremonies, and in its ritual practices, it was said by popular superstition to have called regularly on the Devil and made use of certain biblical verses read backwards, but such embroidery was only to be expected about an apparently magical cult.

Members of the society believed that Cain had been the first horseman. Their traditional toast ran:

Here's to the horse with the four white feet,
The chestnut tail and mane –
A star on his face and a spot on his breast,
And his master's name was Cain.

(The 'four white feet' are a strange reversal of the popular principle we noted previously.)

Initiations of new young members usually took place around Martinmas (11 November) in some such place as an isolated barn, to which they were brought blindfold. Each initiate had to bring a bottle of whisky, a jar of berries or jam, and a loaf of bread.

Still blindfolded, he would be told to 'tak' a grip o' the Old Chiel's hand' and would have a staff thrust into his palm, the end of which was the dried cloven hoof of some animal.

He had to swear to observe the rule 'Hele, conceal, never reveal; neither write, nor dite, nor recite, nor cut, nor carve, nor write in sand.' During the ritual the 'minister' would try to trick him into writing this rule down, and would hit his knuckles with a chain or whip-stock if he fell for it.

When the initiate had been formally accepted, he was taught some of the cult's secrets. For example, one was said to be that if a rider had trouble with his horse, he must take its collar and bridle to a crossroads and recite certain words. (Popular superstition introduced the Devil into this one, too.)

What does seem to be a fact is that many of these secrets were herbal – 'drawing' recipes, which attracted and pleased horses, and 'jading' recipes, which repelled them.

As Doreen Valiente maintains (*An ABC of Witchcraft Past and Present*, p.186): 'These secrets were far from being mere mumbo-jumbo. On the contrary, they consisted of a very thorough and practical knowledge of herbs and other substances which would enable a man to influence horses, if he knew how to use this knowledge.'

Above all, the new member would be told the Word – which is still an unrevealed secret. If this Word was whispered into a horse's ear, it would give the speaker complete control over it.

The Society of the Horseman's Word was but one example of a practice known as 'horse-whispering' – widespread not only in Britain and Ireland, but in similar forms among European gypsies, and in North and South America.

A particularly famous one at the beginning of the nineteenth century was an Irishman called Sullivan. He maintained that horse-whisperers could not explain how the power worked; it was an innate gift. The event that established his reputation concerned a fine but quite unmanageable racehorse belonging to a Colonel Westenra. Sullivan asked to be shut in the stable with the horse, in spite of its savage reputation. He stayed there for about a quarter of an hour and, when he called other people in, he was sitting beside the horse which was lying down quietly. Both horse and man seemed tired, and Sullivan had to be given brandy. The cure of the horse, however, was permanent.

Horse-whisperers were very powerful in Cambridgeshire. The secret phrase they whispered to horses was said to be 'sic jubeo' (I command thus).

Many whisperers used talismans nailed over stable doors as an addition to their repertoire. These included holey-stones, usually of flint, and the shoe or pieces of the hoof of a dead horse to ensure that its offspring inherited its good qualities. Whisperers who did the latter insisted that it bore no relation to the traditional 'lucky horseshoe' charm. The practice still persists in the West Country.

Another favourite piece of equipment was the milt – a spongy substance found in a colt's mouth at birth, and usually swallowed at once. If it could be salvaged in time, a whisperer would treat it with certain aromatic oils, in a traditional ritual. It could then be used as a charm for luring reluctant horses to him.

In Pictish areas, the milt was known as the 'pad'. *Pade* is an Old Pictish word for toad or frog, and the word 'paddock' is still both the common name for a horse's field, and a country name for a frog: 'Paddock ride' means frog spawn, and 'paddock pipes' means marsh horsetail. Of course, the structure on the inside of a horse's hoof is known as the 'frog'. Horse and frog lores overlap mysteriously. See also the technique of the Toadmen on p.95 – a technique which whisperers also often use.

XI *Pictures and Words*

We have spoken much of the Celtic reverence for the horse, but in Britain, its magical and ritual significance seems to have predated the Celtic arrival. Little British art survives from Palaeolithic times, but the only human figure known from that period is on a bone carving found in a Derbyshire cave. The man is wearing a horse mask – and such prehistoric representations of human disguise, experience indicates, refer always to ritual activities.

Moving on to Celtic times, the most famous (and certainly the largest) equine representation in Britain is the White Horse of Uffington, two miles south of the village of that name. It is just off the B4507, from which a side-road leads to a convenient car park. Cut through the turf of the north-west side of a hill of the Berkshire Downs, and into the solid white chalk underneath, it is 360 feet long and 130 feet high. According to the Ministry of Public Works' official notice at the site, it was probably cut by the Belgae, one of the tribal elements of the Celtic incursion; the consensus of opinion dates it about the first century BC.

Its pictorial style, with a somewhat beaked head and a disjointed body, and facing to the right, is very similar to horse-figures found on Gaullish and British coins of around the period, and on two contemporary repoussé buckets discovered at Marlborough and Aylesford.

This beaked characteristic of so many Celtic representations of the horse is also found on the famous Gundestrup Cauldron – a silver bowl dug up in a Danish bog and now in the Danish

National Museum at Copenhagen. One of the Cernunnos-type god figures on it is flanked by two such beaked horses, who are also winged.

Recent investigation of the Uffington site has used a new technique – laser soil dating. This involves bombarding a soil sample with green laser light, and dating its history from the intensity of the blue light which emerges. The investigation established that a terrace had been constructed there for agricultural purposes in about 1000 BC, and that the horse itself was cut about the first century BC. This confirmed its Celtic origin. Also established was that the chalk had not merely been bared, but that chalk had been packed into the dug trenches of the design, and that the original design was considerably less skinny than what has survived.

It has been suggested by some scholars that the horse represents Epona, and that Saxon newcomers later regarded it as sacred to Odin.

Much folklore and legend is attached to the White Horse of Uffington. Weyland's Smithy is in the valley a mile away, and Weyland himself is said to have made its shoes. Standing in the horse's eye with your own eyes closed, turning three times deosil (clockwise), and wishing, will it is claimed make your wish come true 'within a seven'. The number seven appears in another tradition – 'that all places that fall on points calculated in multiples of seven from the Eye are of mystical significance or related to Earth energies' (Murry Hope, *Practical Celtic Magic* p.63).

Is it significant that the number seven was also sacred to the Greek sea god Poseidon, whose totem animal was the horse?

Up to 1897, the Uffington horse was cleaned during a 'scouring festival' by up to 30,000 villagers from miles around every seven years. The festival was marked by games, contests, cheese-rolling, and itinerant stallholders. It is remembered in a country ballad recorded by the Thomas Hughes in his 1857 novel *The Scouring of the White Horse:*

The owld White Horse wants zettin to rights
And the Squire hev promised good cheer,
Zo we'll gee un a scraape to kip un in zhape
And a'll last for many a year.

(Hughes is better known for his novel *Tom Brown's Schooldays*, but this, too, begins in the Vale of the White Horse – 'the nest where the young Browns were hatched'.)

During World War Two the horse was camouflaged to prevent German bombers using it as a navigation landmark. Its cleaning is now the responsibility of the National Trust, who acquired it from the Department of the Environment in 1979.

The antiquity of the Uffington Horse is unquestioned, though scholars may differ over details. Claims for the origin of another famous hill-cut figure, the Westbury Horse, vary from its having been created by King Alfred to celebrate his victory over the Danes, to its being the work of a romantic folly-creating landscaper of the eighteenth century.

The Westbury Horse is cut on the flank of Bratton Down in Wiltshire, and is 182 feet long by 100 feet high. The problem of its origin is greatly complicated by the fact that it was completely redesigned and doubled in size by a Mr Gee, steward to Lord Abingdon, in 1778. Richard Gough, editor of *Camden's Britannia*, had published a drawing of the earlier horse in 1772, very different in appearance from Gee's version – and facing right, instead of left like Gee's (though some argue that the engraver may have reversed Gough's sketch).

All in all, there is now little that is 'magical' about the Westbury Horse. Yet even here there is an interesting query. Bratton Down is crowned by a double-walled hill fort, attributed by folklore to King Alfred. Other hill-cut figures are more often than not overlooked by similar 'forts'. Many experts now doubt whether these structures were military at all, suggesting instead that they were sacred fertility-rite sites, linked in significance to the cut figures below them. 'It may have been these ancient rituals, garbled through the centuries, that formed the basis of the ancient festivals and fairs celebrated in nearby villages up until recent times'. (John Wilcock, *A Guide to Occult Britain*, p.47)

The Red Horse of Tysoe (in fact a group of four, and possibly five, horses of various dates cut in the red clay) certainly carries religious overtones, both pagan and Christian. Unfortunately the figures themselves have disappeared, under ploughing of 1800 and afforestation of 1959, but there are documentary references from 1607, and photographic and excavatory evidence carefully gathered by K.A. Carrdus and W.G. Miller in the 1960s.

Tysoe is in Warwickshire, about eight miles from Banbury near the Stratford road. The word Tysoe means 'spur of land dedicated to Tiw'. Tiw, after whom the English Tuesday is named, was the Teutonic God of success in war, and of agricultural fertility in peacetime (as was the Roman Mars, and doubtless for the same reasons).

The Stour Valley was colonized by the Angles around 600 AD, and they are generally credited with having cut the first Red Horse. Both Tiw and Mars, in their agricultural-fertility aspects, were honoured by rituals around the Spring Equinox – and just north of Tysoe are the Spring and Sunrising Hills. The Tiw and Mars rituals involved the sacrifice of horses – and though there was no such sacrifice in the Tysoe scouring festivals, as Paul Newman puts it (*Gods and Graven Images*, p.70), 'there exist striking points of resemblance in all primitive horse rites'. Newman continues:

> Why, in the case of the Red Horse, the church decreed that Tiw's festival should be reconsecrated as the honouring of Palm Sunday is none too clear. Perhaps, at a loss to correlate the scouring ceremony with anything in their own calendar, they decided to imply that the huge Saxon emblem portrayed the ass on which Christ rode into Jerusalem.

More controversial is a supposed figure at Wandlebury in Cambridgeshire. Wandlebury stands on hills known locally as the Gogs or Gogmagogs. Here various patterns have been recently excavated, the interpretations of which range from their having been naturally formed by glacial action during the last Ice

Age, to the firm conclusion by T.C. Lethbridge (*Witches: Investigating an Ancient Religion*, pp.33 and 89–93) that the earliest of them represents a female figure riding a horse.

The sketch he gives of this figure shows her mounted, with four breasts, and he comments: 'Although the drawing of the original group of Magog and her horse is barbaric, yet it shows a sense of balance and forms a complete picture where it has not been damaged by a later trackway down the side of the hill.'

He interprets the name Ma Gog as meaning 'the Mother Goddess'. He suggests a link (ibid. p.96), both etymologically and in character, with the Irish goddess Macha, who herself was associated with childbirth and with horses.

He also compares the four-breasted Magog with the multi-breasted Diana of Ephesus. Diana (known as Artemis to the Greeks) was a moon goddess, and the horse was one of her totem animals – perhaps because a horse's hoofprint suggests the crescent Moon.

Lethbridge has been called over-imaginative, but if his sketch of the excavation is reasonably accurate, he would seem to have had a strong case for his interpretation of it.

Much smaller than all these – a mere twelve feet long – is the horse cut into the rock of Bidston Hill in Cheshire, near Birkenhead. It faces exactly towards the Midsummer sunrise. Although the present figure is only eighteenth century, there are signs that it was cut to renew an earlier one, and its similarity in style to many of the much older ones, as well as its solar orientation, would seem to confirm this.

The Black Horse of Bush Howe, near Sedburgh in West Yorkshire, is a mysterious image which seems to be regarded locally with a degree of awe and superstition. It is at the head of the remote valley of Long Rigg Beck. It is described as a huge black stallion, rather like the horses in the cave paintings of France and Spain. 'Archaeologists are trying to decide whether the Horse was carved out of the hillside by man, or whether it is a piece of natural erosion' (Guy Ragland Phillips, *Brigantia: A Mysteriography*, p.190).

Phillips himself has seen it clearly, describing it as about 140 yards long and 120 yards high. He has tried to photograph it, but without satisfactory results, and a Ministry of the Environment inspector found it impossible to photograph at all.

Some local people told Phillips: 'Once you have seen it, then you never pass by without looking.' Others, obviously not at ease, said: 'We never saw it; we don't believe it's there.' And one told a woman questioner flatly: 'Never heard of it.'

The long valley points directly towards the sea which is twenty miles away off Morecambe, and tradition says that in the eighteenth century the Black Horse was used as a landmark by smugglers sailing into Morecambe Bay.

Turning to a rather later form of pictorial symbolism – horses occur from time to time in heraldry. One example is the arms of Westphalia, described as 'Gules, a horse courant argent' – in other words, a silver running horse on a red background. This was incorporated as a detail in the arms of Hanover, brought to Britain by George I in 1714, together with lions, but only the lions survived in the British royal arms.

A mounted figure of St George, with his lance piercing the dragon, worn as a pendant to the collar of the Order of the Garter, was added to the insignia of the Order by Henry VIII. A rearing horse is the coat of arms of the county of Kent.

Horse-trappings decorated with heraldic symbol are known as Bardings. Parts of a horse's harness in a coat of arms are described heraldically as Hames or Heames. A Centaur (such as that on the badge of King Stephen) is sometimes described as a Sagittary, recalling its Zodiacal form. A horse with wings is always described as Pegasus.

Spurs and stirrups appear as armorial charges; a single-pointed spur being known as a Pryck-spur, and one with a roundel as a Rouelle-spur.

XII *Visions and Ghosts*

Spectral horses are second only to human ghosts in their frequency, in the stories of many countries. Here in Ireland, they are particularly associated with the *Sidhe* (pronounced 'Shee') or Fairy Folk.

The *Sidhe* play an important part in Irish mythology and folklore. (It is sometimes said that no one in Ireland believes in them, but that everybody is very careful not to offend them!) The aristocracy of the *Sidhe* are the Tuatha Dé Danann (pronounced 'Tooha Day Dahn'n), the Peoples of the Goddess Dana, who is the traditional Mother Goddess of Ireland. The Tuatha were the last occupiers of Ireland before the Gaels, in the mythological cycle, and the memory of them may well have some historical basis, however distorted by legend.

Such legend says that when the invading Gaels conquered Ireland, under the peace settlement the Tuatha retired into the sea and into the hollow hills or *sidhe*-mounds, which they still inhabit as rulers of the Fairy Folk. As befits such an aristocracy, when they emerge from these mounds, they do so mounted.

The Tuatha's reputation for seeming to appear out of the ground, and to disappear just as mysteriously, would accord with the experience the conquerers would have had of the conquered, for the latter would have learned to survive by existing on the fringes, avoiding settlements, and vanishing into the landscape when necessary. As Pennethorne Hughes says (*Witchcraft*, p.77), 'it is perhaps significant that horses should have been so important a feature of fairy mythology when it is remembered that the early peoples were such great horse-breeders'.

Not all accounts of the horse-riding Tuatha, however, are easily put down to faint historical memories embroidered into mythology. Tales of these mounted processions, known as the Hosting of the Sidhe, abound – and not merely among the 'simple-minded'. We have met several people who claim, with apparent sincerity, to have seen them.

One such person was a science student at Trinity College, Dublin, who told us that when he was a boy he used often to see them riding out of a mound near his family home. The Tuatha were on their horses and were accompanied by the lesser orders on foot. They would wave to him as they passed.

'As I grew older, they became more shadowy,' he told us. 'Then a few weeks back, it occurred to me to try an experiment. I borrowed a Geiger counter from college when I visited home, and kept on sitting down in my usual place. Nothing happened for a day or two, then out they came – misty, but acknowledging me as they used to. The Geiger went crazy.'

He gave every impression of believing what he told us, and of being puzzled by it ... Self-induced hallucination? How do you hallucinate a Geiger counter though?

We cannot claim, ourselves, to have seen a Hosting, but when we lived near Ferns in County Wexford, we heard a strange rushing sound outside one night, rather like galloping horses. We could see nothing, but next day Janet mentioned it to a member of our landlord family, good practising Quakers who have lived in the same place for centuries.

'Oh, that'll be the Hosting,' she was told in a completely matter-of-fact voice. 'They pass like the wind.'

Getting in the way of them is apparently inadvisable. Lady Gregory (*Visions and Beliefs in the West of Ireland*, p.212), writing early this century, quoted her informant Simon Neland:

> Late one night I was out walking, and a gun in my hand, and I was going down a little avenue of stones, and I heard after me the noise of a horse's steps. So I stopped and sat down on the stile, for I

> thought the man that's with the horse, I'll have his company a bit of the way. But the noise got louder like as if it was twenty horses coming, and then I was knocked down, and I put out my foot to save the gun from being broken. But when I got up there was no hurt on me or the gun, and the noise was all gone, and the place quiet.

Some time later Neland recounted this experience to his local priest, who had his own interpretation.

> And I said, 'Now would you believe that?' 'I would,' says he. 'And what are such things done by?' says I. 'The fallen angels,' he said, 'for they have power to do such things and to raise wind and storm, but yet they have no hope of salvation at the last.'

This belief seems to have served as a convenient explanation for some. Lady Gregory quotes an old woman from Tyrone as saying: 'Oh, I wouldn't believe in the faeries, but it's no harm to believe in fallen angels!' A Mrs Hynes of Slieve Echtge added a more cheerful note, telling Lady Gregory: 'They can do everything. They can raise the wind, and draw the storm. And to Drogheda they go for wine, for the best wine is in the cellars there.' And one Mike Martin advised: 'It's best to be neighbourly with them anyway – best to be neighbourly.'

Janet has only once actually seen an apparent member of the Tuatha – unmounted, but the incident is worth mentioning in this context. She appeared before Janet standing in a stretch of wild garlic, beautifully but archaically dressed, and spoke to her in what sounded like Old Gaelic. At Janet's heels was a whippet bitch who had been totally blinded in an accident, and who according to the vet was incurable. The whippet jumped up excitedly at the strange figure who stroked her head.

The figure then faded and vanished. Again, sceptics may speak of hallucination, but the fact remains, verified by a surprised vet, that from that day the whippet suddenly recovered ninety per cent of her vision.

One dramatic ghost horse was a near neighbour of ours when we lived outside Drogheda. John Farrell and Margaret Johnson were driving past Lord Dillon's estate at Rath House one night in 1966, when a monstrous horse materialized in front of them, forcing Farrell to brake hard. Miss Johnson described it as 'a huge horse with a man's face and horrible bulging eyes. I could see by John's face that he saw it too ... The animal stretched right across the road and completely blocked the car. It stayed there for nearly two minutes ... We don't drink and two of us couldn't have imagined the same thing.'

This was not the first horse story connected with Rath House. It is said that in the eighteenth century the owner, a Protestant, quarrelled with the parish priest at the door and ordered him off the estate. The priest's horse reared and slammed its hoof down on the doorstep – and the hoofmark can still be seen there.

Knockfierna, a hill in County Limerick, is said to be named after the horse-riding fairy king Donn Firinne. A deep hole in the hillside called Poll na Bruidhne is named as an entrance to his dwelling-place, to which many legends are attached. It was said that if you threw a ball of thread into it, it would be thrown back to you soaked in blood. Donn was not malevolent – he favoured clean farming and kindly spouses, and was as quick to reward good behaviour as to punish bad – but he has always been treated warily. Many reported seeing him riding the countryside at night, sometimes in the sky. So people meeting an anonymous horseman in the dark would cross themselves for safety. The unexplained sound of horse-carriages outside at night was said to be Donn speaking from his cavern.

Spectral horses appear with human ghosts as well as with fairies. Lady Gregory (op. cit. p.193) recalls what a chimney-sweep told her:

> Old Lambert of Dangan was a terror for telling stories; he told me long ago how he was near the Piper's gap on Ballybrit racecourse, and he saw one riding to meet him, and it was old Michael Lynch of Ballybrista, that was dead long before, and he never would go on the racecourse again. And he had heard the car with headless horses driving through Loughrea. From every part they are said to drive, and the place they are all going to is Benmore, near Loughrea, where there is a ruined dwelling-house and an old forth. And at

> Mount Mahon a herd told me the other day he often saw old Andrew Mahon riding about at night. But if I was a herd and saw that I'd hold my tongue about it.

In England, the Wild Hunt tends to replace the Hosting of the Sidhe, and is treated much more warily. In early Saxon terms, it was believed that Odin rode across the sky on winter nights, leading a pack of wild, red-eyed, baying hounds. In the Celtic version, the mounted god leading the Hunt was Herne. Christian interpretations, as one might expect, replaced both gods with the Devil – though one more elaborate version said the Wild Huntsman was a Hebrew who had refused Jesus a cup of water, pointing to the water in a hoofprint and telling him that was good enough for 'such an enemy of Moses'. He was now living out his punishment as a spectre.

The Saxons believed that anyone who saw the Hunt might be carried off to a distant land; and actually to speak to Odin would be fatal.

The Germans tell a similar story of the Black Forest, where a ghostly hunter and his hounds are said to pursue people and animals.

In Fontainebleau Forest in France, the Hunter is known as *Le Grand Veneur*, and is said to be St Hubert, who died in 727. Tradition tells that he was converted to Christianity while hunting on Good Friday and seeing a vision of Christ between the antlers of a stag he was pursuing. He became the patron saint of huntsmen. Considering that the conversion legend did not appear till the fourteenth century, his identification with *Le Grand Veneur* may well be a Christianization of an earlier version.

In some versions of the concept, particular local or national heroes replaced the god (or Devil), and a coach drawn by ghostly horses might substitute for the baying hounds. In one Devonshire belief, for example, Sir Francis Drake drives a team of headless horses pulling a black coach across Dartmoor on stormy moonless nights, and in another from the same area, the

Yeth Hounds or Wish Hounds bay on the wind, hunting the souls of unbaptized babies. Windsor Great Park is one place where Herne's Wild Hunt is often said to manifest.

King Arthur, of course, makes a similar if less frightening appearance. He is said to be seen on Midsummer Eve leading a troop of mounted knights down Cadbury Hill in Somerset, the legendary location of his court of Camelot.

The ghost of England's most notorious highwayman, Dick Turpin, rides his horse Black Bess in many places, right up to the Scottish border. In particular, Turpin and Bess are said to haunt the neighbourhood of the Old Swan Inn at Woughton on the Green in Buckinghamshire, which he often used as his headquarters. At Loughton in Epping Forest there is a grim addition – he rides down Traps Hill with the ghost of a woman clinging to his back, whom he tortured and murdered for her money.

An even more gruesome memory of a highwayman concerns eighteenth-century Clibbon the Pieman, of Datchworth, Hertfordshire. The locals regarded him as a friend, till they discovered he was a highwayman who had robbed many of them. Furious, they beat him up and then tied his half-senseless body to a horse to be dragged along the ground to Woolmer Green, where they finished him off. People passing along this route in the evenings have seen the ghost of a horse pulling a writhing body behind it, with the victim crying out for mercy. Other witnesses have heard all the sounds, while seeing nothing.

Another Datchworth haunting involves a horse and cart, but strangely, only the cart can be seen. It concerns a local memory of the eviction from their home of a debt-ridden family, the Eaves, who died in the village poorhouse in 1769. Their bodies were piled in a cart and carried to the churchyard for burial. Locals and visitors have seen a spectre of this procession – yet always only of the cart, moving of its own accord; both the horse and the bodies remain invisible.

Yet another Datchworth ghost horse is commemorated by the name of the White Horse Inn at Burnham Green. He belonged to a Civil War Royalist in Welches Farm, who was caught by the Cromwellians and beheaded, his head being stuck on a spike in his stable yard. The soldiers then tried to take his stallion, but the animal resisted them, so they decapitated him too, and its headless ghost has been seen galloping along the road nearby.

A mounted ghost who rides around Great Park at Ampthill in Bedfordshire has been seen by many people, including a policeman on holiday. He is described as a knight in full armour with a plumed helmet and riding a white horse.

A keen horsewoman who was thrown and killed on a morning canter at Loakes Road in High Wycombe, Buckinghamshire, during the seventeenth century has often been seen riding furiously and always disappearing at the same spot.

No historical event explains a haunting in Chinthurst Woods, at Bramley near Guildford in Surrey where an old gypsy woman is often seen leading a shabby brown horse, but one selective viewing of them is rather strange. In June 1971 an airline pilot was driving his daughter through the woods when he saw the pair and, thinking they were 'real', said 'I wonder where they're going' – and found that his daughter could only see the horse. He was still puzzling over this when woman and horse both vanished.

One of the most haunted villages in England is Prestbury in Gloucestershire, a couple of miles outside Cheltenham. At least six different phenomena are regarded as commonplace by the locals, who are apparently unperturbed by them. One ghost frequently seen there, and heard galloping, is believed to be that of a Royalist despatch rider, who was bearing news to Cheltenham of Cromwell's victory at Worcester but was killed by an arrow before he could deliver it.

Another Civil War haunting, again mounted, has occasionally been seen on the banks of the Wye by Goodrich Castle in Herefordshire. The story is that the castle was under siege in 1646 by Cromwellian Colonel Birch. His niece Alice was in love with Clifford, one of the defenders, and managed to enter the castle and join him. When the castle was about to fall, the couple broke through the crowd of attackers on horseback and tried to ford the Wye, but it was flooded and swept them away. Their bodies were never found, but several people on stormy nights have seen the triple spectre of a man on horseback with a lady mounted behind him, trying to force the horse through the river.

Rarely, the ghost appearance of a horse is believed to represent a dead human being. Cranmere Pool in North Dartmoor is now drained, but it used to be a dreadful bog in which evil spirits were said to be consigned. A black pony who still occasionally appears there is believed in fact to be the ghost of Bengie Geare, a former mayor of Okehampton.

Back to highwaymen – or should we say highwaypersons? A famous one was Lady Katherine Ferrers, respectable aristocrat by day and secret robber by night, on whose story the Margaret Lockwood film *The Wicked Lady* was based. The Wicked Lady pub at Nomansland, near St Albans, Hertfordshire, is named after Lady Ferrers, and she is said to haunt the place. The landlord, Douglas Payne, however, told the *Herts Advertiser* that in December 1970 he had had another experience which was confirmed by the behaviour of his dog. Walking on the nearby common, he heard the sound of a horse galloping very fast. It seemed to pass so close he could have touched it, but he could see nothing. It took quite a time to quieten his badly frightened dog.

Pig Lane at Abingdon, Berkshire, is haunted by an eighteenth-century squire furiously driving a coach and pair to trample and kill the peasant lover of his daughter – which in reality he apparently succeeded in doing, bloodily.

A coach and four haunts the grounds of Antrim Castle in Northern Ireland, though in this case it was the driver and passengers who were the victims. The haunting only occurs on 31 May, which is the anniversary of the accident. The driver was drunk, and mistaking the reflection of the moon in the Long Pond for the road surface, he drove straight into the water, where the people and horses all drowned. The ghostly coach is seen disappearing into the same pond.

A Surrey coach-and-four apparition haunts a pathway near the A22 road at Riddlesdown, Kenley. Local tradition explains it by the fact that the pathway follows the line of the old coach road from Purley to Kenley, and says it recalls a fatal accident that happened there just before the new road was opened in the nineteenth century. The ghost team always vanishes just before the pathway rejoins the A22.

Another coach accident off the A22 is said to explain a haunting on the B269 at Warlingham, Surrey. In the late 1840s, a highwayman frightened the horses of a coach team, who veered off the road into a pond where the driver and passengers were all drowned. A coach has been seen in this same pond, 'all lit up, with passengers screaming at the windows.'

A coach-and-team drowning by the Old Court House at Shelsley Walsh, Worcestershire, the apparition of which was reported by witnesses in 1965, dates back to Henry VIII's reign. Lady Lightfoot, who lived there, had offended the King by her outspoken criticisms of his policies. Friends and relatives, knowing she was in danger, sent a coach and four one Christmas Eve in an attempt to rescue her, but somehow the team ended up in the moat – perhaps the driver was drunk – and the rescue failed. The witnesses of the haunting, who knew nothing of this story, had seen a large vague shape racing across the lawn and plunging into the moat, but could find nothing where it had disappeared. (King Henry won, by the way: the imprudent Lady Lightfoot was murdered.)

A nineteenth-century Welsh coaching accident which has since been seen by several witnesses happened during a storm on the Abergavenny Road, Monmouth. It seems that the horses were panicked by lightning and, being unable to stop on a sharp corner, crashed into a wall, killing themselves and flinging the passengers over into a field. The ghostly 'replay' of this tragedy always stops as the wreckage of the coach reaches the ground.

At Longcompton in Warwickshire a coach and six are occasionally seen careering down Harrow Hill, the driver and horses all being headless. As they are only seen during or after a heavy winter rainstorm, they may well recall another bad-weather accident. This one is said to have happened in the seventeenth or eighteenth century.

Heard but not seen is a coach and team on the road outside the William the Fourth Inn at Ewell in Surrey. It seems to start up, and then to move off towards London. The road was once a regular coaching route, and although the inn itself dates from the reign it was named after, medieval and Roman remains prove that the site is very much older.

Andrew Green, whose fascinating book *Our Haunted Kingdom* records some of these and many other such hauntings, reports on pp.329-30 one incident that he experienced himself at Winchelsea in Sussex. He was about to turn his car on to a main road, when he heard 'what sounded like a large number of horses galloping up the hill from Rye. He reversed back into the side road to let them pass, but when it sounded as though they were only yards away, all was suddenly silent. He drove out slowly, but no animals were anywhere in sight. When he mentioned this to the proprietress of his hotel, she told him many motorists had experienced the same, and that it was said to be connected with the Weston brothers – highwaymen who had terrorized the district and were caught and executed in 1782. The headless ghost of George Weston had often been seen waiting under a tree near the spot where Andrew Green had heard the galloping.

Mrs Patricia Nicholson, mother-in-law of showjumper Eddie Machen, who is a close neighbour of Janet's, tells her how the ghost of a groom often appears around the stables of their old estate. She also tells how friends of hers in the West of Ireland sometimes hear the sound of a coach and horses coming up their drive at night. When they look out, there is nothing to be seen, but next morning there are wheel- and hoof-marks clearly visible in the gravel of the drive.

For reasons which are difficult to pin down, many ghost horses appear headless. One such haunted the road outside the first house we lived in in Ireland, close to Ferns in County

Wexford. It had belonged to Colonel Buckey, a notorious late eighteenth-century English officer who tyrannized the rebellious Irish locals, and burned down nearby Boolavogue Church, killing the men, women and children who had taken refuge there. His headquarters was Rockspring, the farm owned by our landlords, a Quaker family whose ancestors of Buckey's time had secretly helped the rebels.

Buckey met his death on horseback, when a low-hanging branch caught and broke his neck. Both he and his horse haunt the road. In the circumstances, one would expect Buckey to be the headless one, but it is the horse who appears thus. We ourselves never saw the horse, though we knew people who had. Janet did, however, meet the ghost of the unsavoury Buckey, and was not sorry when he faded away.

Another horse who caused his master's deserved death, though in this case years after its own, was that of Sir Roger de Shurland, Lord of the Isle of Sheppey in Kent in 1300. Sir Roger killed a monk who defied him, and was pursued by the county sheriff. He managed to escape by swimming out on horseback into the Thames estuary where Edward I's ship was passing, and obtaining the King's pardon.

Back on shore, he was confronted by an old woman who prophesied that the horse, having saved his life, would also cause his death. Sir Roger promptly drew his sword and beheaded the horse. Years afterwards, he came across the skull while he was walking on the beach, and kicked it angrily. One of the teeth penetrated his boot, causing an infection in his foot from which he soon died.

Sir Roger's tomb is still in Minster Abbey church on Sheppey, bearing his effigy, with a horse's head by its right foot.

The word 'nightmare' is interesting, both etymologically and psychologically. The *Shorter Oxford English Dictionary* gives the following two-part definition:

> 1. A female monster supposed to settle upon people and animals in their sleep producing a feeling of suffocation. 2. A feeling of

> suffocation or great distress felt during sleep, from which the sleeper vainly tries to free himself; a bad dream producing these or similar sensations 1562.

The '1562' dates the first known example of that particular meaning. The two definitions are in accord with the gradual shift in ordinary thinking about such things – in this case from explaining the phenomenon by a possessive evil demon, to seeing it in terms of an anxiety with which one has not come to terms.

Oddly enough, the element 'mare' in 'nightmare' comes, via Middle English, from a different Old Teutonic root than 'mare' meaning a female horse. The other meaning is found in the Saxon Mara or Mare, a dream-demoness of the type we have described, who had the additional attribute of guarding hidden treasure like a hen guards her eggs – hence the expression 'mare's nest', for a hoped-for gain which turns out to be a mere dream.

Up to the early sixteenth century, in English, the difference survived, and a separate meaning of 'mare' was a spectre or hag. The subconscious confusion of the two took hold, however. The concept of the oppressive monster being a female horse, its weight and strength being more than one can handle, remained below the threshold of consciousness.

There was another ambivalence here, between the suffocating female monster of the *OED*'s meaning 1, and the medieval concept of the succubus – a female demon who seduced men in their sleep (the male equivalent who seduced women being the incubus). The ingrained Church aversion to sex and the 'lusts of the flesh' must have made the borderline between forbidden eroticism and the suffocating female monster impossible to define; and what could be a more vivid symbol of a female who was at the same time both fascinating and terrifying, than the Mare?

XIII *Stubborn Survivals*

Seasonal festivals and rituals are an integral part of all human cultures, religions, and folk patterns. Round the year – particularly in Celtic countries or in those, like England, where the Celtic strain is a persistent component – horses play a significent role in the cycle. We have already examined some aspects of this in Chapter VIII.

Midsummer fires, and the folk customs connected with them, are still widespread in Ireland. The traditional date for them in some areas is St John's Eve on 23 June, and in others 28 June, the eve of St Peter and St Paul's Day, sometimes called 'Little Bonfire Night'. When we lived on a lonely coastal stretch of County Mayo, in the far West, we could see twinkling bonfires from horizon to horizon as the darkness set in on St John's Eve.

Jumping over the glowing ashes of the dying Midsummer fire was (and in places still is) a lucky act, helping the unmarried to find husbands or wives, pregnant women to have safe deliveries, travellers to have safe journeys, and so on. Driving cattle and horses over them, or between two such fires, ensured the livestock's health, and in the case of cattle, a good milk yield.

In one local Irish ritual, still surviving in the last century, the horse was the symbol, not of itself, strangely enough, but of the cattle. A man wearing a horse's head, and concealed under a white sheet, jumped the fire and chased the watchers, who greeted it with laughter and shouts of 'white horse!' This dummy horse was said to represent all the cattle.

Few popular rituals are more persistent than those connected with the last sheaf of a harvest. It may be called the Maiden, the Maidenhead, the Head, the Bride, the Oats-Bride, or the Wheat-Bride, and is often cut by the youngest girl present. (In Germany, the girl herself often shares the title.) Carried in procession by the harvester the sheaf is presented to the farmer's wife. She dresses it up like a woman, decorates it with ribbon, and hangs it in her kitchen.

In Aberdeenshire, the farmer's wife keeps the Maiden until the first mare foals, when she presents it to the mare as her first food after the birth. Centuries of belief have maintained that failure to do this will not only harm the foal, but will have a deleterious effect on the prosperity of the farm as a whole.

In many places, the corn-spirit is envisaged as a horse or mare. In parts of Germany, a crop bending before the wind is greeted with 'There runs the Horse!' and the last sheaf of oats is called 'the Oats-stallion'.

In parts of Scandinavia, a Christmas sheaf is attached to the ridge of a house or barn. Danish children call this sheaf 'Santa Claus's horse'. Originally, tradition maintains, it was regarded as Odin's horse Sleipnir.

(The replacement of the horse by the reindeer in the Santa Claus legend originated, oddly enough, in America during Christmas 1822, when a children's poem written by Dr Clement Clarke Moor, *The Visit of St Nicholas*, became widely popular. It described St Nicholas arriving on a miniature sleigh drawn by eight reindeer. Before long, the reindeer image of Santa Claus's transport spread to Europe, where it has virtually replaced St Nicholas's horse, except in Germany and Austria.)

Back to the last corn-sheaf. In Hertfordshire, the custom is for this sheaf to be bound together while it is still standing, and for it to be named 'the Mare'. The harvesters call back and forth to each other in a ceremony known as 'crying the Mare'. When the first farm has completed its harvest, the Mare corn-spirit is regarded as being moved on to the next, and so on. The last farm to receive the Mare is looked on as being a laggard. Similar traditions are found in Shropshire.

The same identification of the corn-spirit with the horse is found in the Lille area of France. The first sheaf of the harvest is bound to a cross of boxwood called 'the cross of the horse', and taken to the barn for the youngest horse to tread on it. The last sheaf is known as 'the remains of the horse', and is given to the youngest horse of the village to eat.

An important ritual horse in Ireland used to be the Lair Bhan (White Mare), who had links with May Day, Christmas, but most particularly with Hallowe'en, when in County Cork and elsewhere her retinue went from farmhouse to farmhouse, blowing cows' horns and chanting verses. Farmers greeted the procession with gifts of produce, to ensure the farms' prosperity for the coming year. (In the ancient Celtic calendar, the New Year, and winter, begins on 1 November. It was a two-season year with the summer beginning on 1 May. This pattern was typical of the cattle- and horse-raising economy.)

The horse's or stag's skull on a stick, often with the bottoms of bottles as eyes, and carried by a man shrouded in a sheet, was a common feature of pagan seasonal rituals long after the imposition of Christianity. First known ecclesiastical mention of it was by the Bishop of Barcelona in 370 AD. St Augustine (354–430 AD) forbade 'the filthy practice of dressing up like a horse or a stag'. The official ban and the popular practice both persisted through the centuries, and the 'Hobby Horse' is a feature of many local seasonal festivals which still survive.

In England, either the Twelve Days of Christmas or Hallowe'en was the time for the appearance of the Hodening Horse, or in Kent the Hooden Horse – again, a man (the 'Hoodener') under a sheet manipulating a horse's head. The head was sometimes made of wood, but often it was an actual horse's skull. He was accompanied by a groom, a jockey trying to ride it, a 'Mollie' – (a man dressed as a woman and carrying a besom) – and a group of musicians. Here, too, the party went from house to house and was greeted with gifts. On the way, the Hooden Horse would make a play of chasing girls, and the groom of restraining him.

His appearance could scare nervous people, especially at night when he started his rounds. At Broadstairs in 1839, one woman suddenly confronted by him died of fright, and as a result the local magistrates banned the custom in the town. In general, however, he was welcomed as a herald of fertility and good fortune.

The horse's mouth (whether the head was wooden or a skull) could be opened and closed by the operator pulling strings, and bystanders would put coins in it. One Kentish song for these processions was:

Three jolly hodening boys
Lately from town;
For apples or for money
We search the country round.

At Reculver, and possibly in other Kentish parishes, only men who worked with horses during the year were allowed to be part of the Hodening team.

Hodening had died out in Kent, but it has recently been revived in one or two places. At Folkestone the Hooden Horse now collects for charity at Christmas, accompanied by handbell ringers. Since 1954 he has appeared in Charing at Whitsun, associated with the Morris Men who dance from the chancel of the church to the market square. At Wickambreaux near Canterbury, the village inn was renamed the Hooden Horse in 1956. In early September, the time of the hop harvest, Morris Men and handbell ringers circulate in the village and end up at the inn.

Hodening Horses were found in other counties – for example around Doncaster in Yorkshire and are associated with the Christmas Mummers.

A similar custom to Hodening is found in Germany, called the *Schimmel* ('white horse'). One variant there is for several boys to join together to form a horse, which another boy rides.

Another English house-to-house procession involving a dummy horse took place in Cheshire villages at Hallowe'en.

The horse was known as Dick, Dicky Tatton, Dobby Horse, or Young Ball, and he too was a girl-chaser who had to be restrained. This Cheshire procession included a mummers' play known as 'soul caking', with the typical mummers' plot of a fight to the death and a magical revival. Janet and Colin Bord (*Earth Rites*, p.202) tell us: 'The only current performance of this soul caking play takes place at Antrobus in Cheshire and is a 1926 revival after a lapse of some fourteen years. The team no longer visits the wealthier farms and big houses, but tours the pubs by car.'

At Higher Whitley in Cheshire, after the soul-caking play was over, the Hodeners would bury the horse's skull with a mock funeral. A turn-of-the-century Hodening skull found at Whitley about 1935 was saved from destruction by A.W. Boyd of Frandley, and presented to Manchester Museum.

A South Wales door-to-door wooden-headed horse was known as Mari Llwyd (grey mare), who made her processions around Christmas, Boxing Day and the New Year, accompanied by various characters including Punch and Judy. The procedure here was to sing verses at the door, which were answered from inside, lapsing into an exchange of witty insults; whoever dried up first, lost, and if the door was that of a pub and Mari Llwyd's party won, drinks were on the house. Some innkeepers at the turn of the century, it is said, hired poets for the occasion to improve their chances. Mari Llwyd was supposed to be a mare, but she too chased the girls – in this case being beaten off them by Judy with her broom.

The horse-head jaws were often hinged to bite, and part of the fun was for the operator to try to catch people with them. Anyone so caught had to pay a forfeit to be released.

A traditional explanation of Mari Llwyd (or a Christian attempt to make her respectable) was that she was a mare who had to be turned out of the Bethlehem stable to make room for the Holy Family, and has been roaming the world looking for shelter ever since.

Mari Llwyd procession still survive in a few Glamorgan and

Carmarthen villages. Some folklorists associate the Mari Llwyd custom wih Robin Hood's Maid Marian, while others believe that like Santa Claus's horse in Denmark, it derives originally from Odin's Sleipnir.

Boxing Day, 26 December, a favourite day for Mari Llwyd customs, is also St Stephen's Day (as it is always called in Ireland). In Sweden, it is marked by horse parades and races, in honour of their own Stephen who was martyred in the ninth century, and who was a lover of horses. On that day, horses are given consecrated corn and salt, or sprinkled with holy water.

The most famous wooden-headed horse ritual in the British Isles is of course that of the 'Obby 'Oss at Padstow in Cornwall. The town is decorated on May Eve with flags and a flower-decked maypole in the town centre. From midnight to about 2 a.m., the people of Padstow walk through the town singing the Night Song.

Unite and unite and let us all unite,
  For summer is acome unto day.
And whither we are going we will all unite,
  In the merry morning of May.

I warn you young men every one
To go into the greenwood and fetch your May home.

Appropriate verses are sung at the doors of the various houses they pass, such as:

Arise up Mr—, and joy you betide,
And bright is your bride that lies by your side.

Arise Mrs— and gold be your ring,
And give to us a cup of ale the merrier we shall sing.

At 10 a.m. on May Day, one of the two 'Osses – the Blue 'Oss – emerges from his stable. An hour later, the older Red 'Oss appears. (The colours refer to the sashes and ribbons worn by the escorts, not to the 'Osses themselves.) Each 'Oss is enacted by a man wearing a big circular bell-shaped frame covered with black oilskin. The man's head sticks out of the top, wearing a pointed hat; he manipulates a carved horse's head in front, and has a horsetail behind.

The 'Oss is led by a dancer or teaser waving a shield-shaped 'club', with which he or she encourages the 'Oss to prance and gyrate through the town's lanes. Also escorting him are Mayers playing accordions and drums, while the crowd shout ' 'Oss, 'Oss, wee 'Oss!'

The Day Song resumes the door-to-door calling:

Arise up Mr—, I know you well and fine,
You have a shilling in your purse and I wish it were in mine.

Where are the maidens that here now should sing?
They are in the meadows, the flowers gathering.

The usual girl-chasing is involved: here the 'Oss tries to capture them under his skirt. To be captured thus is good luck; it means the girl will soon find a husband, or have a baby, if she is already married.

The girl-chasing element, which as we have seen is almost universal in such horse rituals, is not a mere romp. It expresses the age-old significance of the horse as a symbol of fertility, whether it is the potency of the stallion or the fecundity of the mare. In the magical thinking which underlies folk customs, the symbol and its ritual enactment evoke the desired fact which the symbol represents.

Another deeply significant element is found in the Padstow ritual – the theme of death and rebirth. Every now and then the Mayers' music becomes solemn, and the Day Song becomes the Dirge:

O where is St George, O where is he–O?
He's in his long boat all on the salt sea–O.
Up flies the kite, down falls the lark–O,
Aunt Ursula Birdhood she had an old yow,
And she died in her own Park–O.

(A fuller text of the Night Song, Day Song and Dirge may be found in Murry Hope's *Practical Celtic Magic*, pp.169–171. She points out that the words appear to have changed considerably over the years, and adds: 'Bearing in mind the antiquity of the verses and the energy overlays they have accumulated over the centuries, this is not surprising.')

When the Dirge is being sung, the 'Oss sinks to the ground and pretends to die. The tempo changes, the drums roll, and the Mayers bring him back to life with a return to the Day Song.

St George features in many such rituals of slaying and resurrection, particularly in Christmas mumming plays. His name is a Christian label on a very much older pagan concept. In the midwinter rituals, he represents the Oak King, God of the Waxing Year, who slays the Holly King, God of the Waning Year, and immediately cries out that he has killed his brother. In the mumming plays, the Holly King is represented by the Turkish knight (another Christian label to signify the opponent). The doctor then appears with his magic bag, and the slain twin is resurrected to universal rejoicing.

Interestingly, the hill next to the White Horse of Uffington is called Dragon Hill, and local legend says that it was here that St George slew the dragon. The patches where grass will not grow are said to be where the dragon's blood was spilled.

In Cheshire, the mummers of Antrobus, Comberbach, Acton Bridge and other villages perform basically the same play, though at Hallowe'en, and with King George replacing St George, and the Black Prince of Paradise replacing the Turkish knight. These Cheshire mummers, however, add two other characters – the wild horse and his driver, who play an active part in the story.

These mentions of St George (or King George – obviously a corruption of the same name) point to underlying identity between such seasonal horse folk-customs and the age-old ritualization of the fertility cycle of the year.

In Romania, morris dancers – who are closely related to mummers – are called *calusari*, and *calus* means 'little horse'.

The Tale of Taliesin, a riddling poem by the ninth-century Welsh bard of that name, contains a hint of what may have been a Winter Solstice ritual involving horses.

In a horse-race described at the end of the poem, Taliesen tells how he helped Prince Elphin's jockey to beat the twenty-four horses of King Maelgwn on the plain of Rhiannon. He charred twenty-four holly twigs, and Elphin's jockey used these to strike each of the King's horses as he overtook them.

Robert Graves (*The White Goddess*, p.420) interprets this particular passage as symbolizing the end of the reign of the Holly King. 'The horses represent the last twenty-four hours of the Old Year, ruled over by the Holly King, which (with the help of destructive magic) the Divine child puts behind him one by one.'

Perhaps the most ancient religious concept of all, reflected in countless myths and rituals, is that of the immortality of the Earth-Mother Goddess, but the annual death, as his virility begins to wane, of the Son-Lover God who fertilizes her – followed by his resurrection with restored potency.

The sacrificed and resurrected God is a central theme of most religions, including Christianity. One must allow Christians the right to claim that they have transformed the theme to a higher spiritual level, but even they attune its ritualization to the cycle of the year, with Jesus' birth (undated in Scripture or history) celebrated at the Winter Solstice, and his sacrifice and resurrection at the flowering of Spring.

At the grass-roots level of folk custom, however, on which 'official' religion often has only a surface effect, the ancient concepts linger. To embody the eternal cycle of death, rebirth and fertilization – what symbol is more vividly appropriate than the horse?

A strange Easter Monday ritual survived in Ashton-under-Lyne, Lancashire, until just before World War Two. It was called Riding the Black Lad, or the Black Knight. The effigy of a knight in black armour and cloak was paraded on horseback through the packed streets of the town, escorted by musicians and by a company of young men mounted or on foot to represent his retainers. At an open space, the effigy was taken off the horse, pelted with stones and other missiles, and finally shot to pieces with guns.

According to local tradition, the Black Lad represented Sir Ralph de Assheton, a fifteenth-century knight who shared with his brother Robin the right of 'guld-riding' in the district which was a medieval custom intended to encourage good farming. Individuals empowered to exercise the right could inspect lands annually, and fine or punish tenants who allowed weeds to grow on them. Sir Ralph, the story goes, became hated for using his powers with great severity. 'Other tyrannies also have been ascribed to him, but these are probably later embroideries of the original tale' (Christina Hole, *British Folk Customs*, p.164).

In the end, according to the tradition, he was killed in the streets of Ashton by someone he had offended. The inspection right was subsequently abolished, and the annual riding was said to commemorate both Sir Ralph's death and the abolition.

Christina Hole (ibid. p.165) concludes from various evidence 'That this is the true explanation of the custom is very unlikely'. She suggest that Sir Ralph's unpopularity attached his legend to an already existing custom, the effigy perhaps originally representing the hunger of winter being driven out in spring.

A similar Easter Monday ritual, called Riding the Lord, existed at Neston in Cheshire till the mid-nineteenth century. In this, a man was paid to ride a donkey the whole length of the village street while people pelted him with rotten eggs and other rubbish. No local explanation was given of this, however, even to nineteenth-century inquirers, apart from 'that's always been done'. The hired scapegoat probably also represented the banished evils of winter, or the end of the Lenten fast.

In County Kerry, the Great White Horse came out to honour the midsummer sun. It was a skull-and-pole horse, eight feet high, with its bearer covered by the usual sheet. Like its English counterparts, it chased girls – and as always in Ireland, it jumped the midsummer fire to ensure fertility and good fortune.

The equivalent of the hobby horse is found in many other lands. In France it is known as *le cheval-jupon*. At Lanz in Navarre it is associated with a giant. There are many examples of it in the Basque lands, both French and Spanish, where it is accompanied by musicians and singers.

In Belgium, hobby horses accompany many seasonal processions, but they seem to have lost the ritual significance they have retained elsewhere.

In Upper Murthal in the Austrian Alps, the Schimmel, or white hobby horse, is put up for sale at the end of the springtime festivities, and shakes itself to pieces at the feet of its generous buyer.

In the Slovenian Alps, the hobby horse is called Rusa, and its head and neck are covered with porcupine quills. It, too, is a spring festival horse, and a collector of money.

In Bohemia and Moravia, the hobby horses are very large, requiring three men under the sheet to carry them. They are paraded on St Nicholas' Day, 6 December, at spring festivals, and (as in many other European places) at weddings. They, like so many others, are girl-chasers.

One of Poland's many hobby horses, at Cracow, is said to commemorate a victory over a Tartar invasion. The horse is dressed as a Tartar, and at one point in its procession it lies down briefly in front of the bishop's palace, presumably to symbolize the Tartar defeat.

In a village comedy ritual at Madura in southern India, a man dressed as a woman is robbed as 'she' sleeps. Two hobby horses appear, and one abducts the 'woman', refusing to allow anyone near her. Other versions of this are found, many of them connected with weddings and with the local deity.

Langholm in Dumfriess-shire was one of the Scottish border towns which used to suffer most from English raids, and it still celebrates its continued freedom on the last Friday in July with a horseback procession known as the Common Riding. A young man is chosen as Cornet for the year. He rides up a steep hill, followed by his mounted supporters. They carry several traditional symbols, while the Cornet leads them along a centuries-old route through the town. Other border towns have similar Common Ridings, but Langholm's is one of the oldest.

(Incidentally, this area was the headquarters of the Armstrong clan, famous for their cattle-rustling by moonlight – a meaningful local saying was 'There will be moonlight again'. So it is appropriate that when Neil Armstrong, the first man to walk on the moon, visited Langholm in 1972, they made him a Freeman of the town.)

Gypsies still have their own 'horse magic'. Sybil Leek, in *Diary of a Witch* (pp.68–72), tells of her friends the New Forest gypsies, and of some of the tricks they used in handling and profiting from the local ponies, when she was a young girl. The New Forest ponies are about fourteen hands and very compact. They are said to be the descendants of ponies which swam ashore from Spanish Armada ships sunk in the English Channel. The gypsies describe them as 'black gold whinnying in the hedgerows'.

One trick, which its practitioner described to Sybil as 'magic', made a pony which he had sold for a good price to a gorgio (non-gypsy) find its own way back to him again and again, till at last the exasperated gorgio sold it back to him for half the original price. The 'magic' consisted of making a paste from certain herbs, and then mixing a tiny square of the paste with the pony's favourite herbage, such as clover. The gypsy would put the square under his armpit for several days to absorb his perspiration, and feed it to the pony just before he sold it. The pony then kept coming back for more. 'The trick,' Sybil assured us, 'never failed.'

Other tricks, used at Salisbury racecourse, could make horses win or lose races. A gorse-bush thorn inserted in the delicate part under the horse's tail would make it shoot ahead in a short race, while a whistle too highly-pitched for human hearing, blown at the right spot and moment, would make a horse swerve enough to lose his place.

From the New Forest gypsies, Sybil 'learned just about everything a woman should not know about horses'.

Horse references are still an element in English metaphor and slang: 'a horse of a different colour', 'flogging a dead horse', 'get off your high horse,' and so on. Now that horses are no longer a part of daily life for the majority, however, many of these usages have died out.

The simple noun 'horse' used to mean various things in colloquial speech. In the eighteenth century, it meant a lottery ticket hired out by the day, or in London, a day's leave of absence from the Fleet debtors' prison (and also, with a capital H, the Horsemonger Lane gaol); or in workmen's jargon, work charged for before it was completed (the unprofitable remainder being 'dead horse') In the late eighteenth century, in bargees' talk, 'horse' meant a mud bank – in the sense that if you were 'riding' it when the tide fell, you had to stay 'in the saddle' till it rose again.

The verb 'to horse' used to mean to mate with a woman, to flog, or to outdo another workman at piece-work.

From the sixteenth to the eighteenth century, 'as good as a shoulder of mutton for a sick horse' meant utterly useless or worthless.

'As holy as a horse' in the sixteenth century meant excessively pious, and in nineteenth century tailors' slang, for some reason, a 'horse-Protestant' was a churchman.

Nautical usages were many. Till the mid-nineteenth century, an arrogant or supercilious officer was known as a 'horse', and an unpopular officer was a 'horsy-face'. A 'salt-horse squire' was a warrant officer (from the nautical phrase 'salt horse for salted beef'. 'Horse-boxes', up to the First World War, meant senior military officers' cabins on a naval ship.

The 'horse latitudes' were that part of the Atlantic north of the trade winds, in which winds were notoriously unpredictable. This probably came from the Spanish 'golfo de las yeguas' (gulf of the mares) for the tricky waters between Spain and the

Canaries, compared with 'golfo de las damas' (of the ladies) for the waters from the Canaries to the West Indies, which were generally calm and favourable.

In army slang, 'horse-milliner' was a dandified but inefficient trooper, and among bandsmen, a 'horse's leg' was a bassoon. 'Put the saddle on the right horse' used to mean to apportion blame accurately.

In the fifteenth and sixteenth centuries, 'come for horse and harness' meant to pursue one's own interests. From the seventeenth to the early twentieth century, 'they cannot hitch (or stable or set) their horses together' meant they cannot agree.

Cockney rhyming slang came into it, too. 'Horse and trap' meant gonorrhoea (clap), and 'horse and cart' meant heart.

In sexual slang, 'horse-collar' or 'horse-shoe' meant the female genitals; a 'horse-kiss' or 'horse-buss' was a rough or resounding kiss; 'horse-godmother' meant a big masculine woman; and a 'horse-leech' was a whore (or by extension, an extortionate person or miser).

In the nineteenth century, a 'horse-breaker' was a woman hired to ride in the park – often with connotation that she was *demi-monde* infiltrating polite society. An alternative explanation, given by *The Times* for using the phrase 'a pretty horse-breaker' for such a woman, was that she was anonymous or nameless in society, and the first-known woman called Anonyma was a famous equestrian. The word Incognita (unknown or unrecognized) was also applied to such an infiltrator.

'Horse-capper', 'horse-courser', or 'horse-chaunter' all meant a dealer in worthless horses, or horses that had been tampered with. A 'horse-duffer' was one who altered the brands on stolen horses.

'A horse foaled on an acorn' meant the gallows – or in the army, the triangle of crossed halberds under which soldiers were flogged.

'To send for a horse-ladder' was to send someone on a fool's errand – like the more modern phrase 'send for a left-handed screwdriver'. The term 'horse-marines' was sarcastically used to mean an imaginary corps – 'do you think we belong to the horse-marines?'

'To fall away from a horse-load to a cart-load', from the seventeenth to the early nineteenth century, meant to put on weight suddenly. 'Horse-lop', was a pudding of plumless suet. In sporting slang, 'horse to a hen' meant long odds. 'Horse-nails', till the middle of the last century, meant money. 'To knock somebody into horse-nails' meant to defeat him soundly, while 'to feed on horse-nails', in cribbage, meant playing to keep down your opponent's score rather than to increase your own. 'Running before your horse to market' meant counting your chickens before they were hatched.

XIV *Honours List*

To end with, here is a list of individual horses famous in legend and fairy-tale, or in fiction which has achieved legendary status (such as Cervantes' *Don Quixote*). Some of them, such as Alexander the Great's mount Bucephalos, existed historically, but their reputation has been sufficiently expanded by myth and folklore (or, like Caligula's horse Incitatus, were sufficiently bizarrely treated) to qualify them for inclusion in a book on horse-magic.

There are several references here to horses of the Aesir in Norse mythology, because their horses always tended to be named. The Aesir were the gods and goddesses associated with Odin. Basically they were those of the mounted warrior aristocracy, who subordinated the Vanir, which were the deities associated with Thor and revered by the seafarers and peasantry. In later years the two tended to merge into one pantheon, but the Aesir remained the only mounted ones.

ABASTER: ('Away from the Stars') and ABATOS ('Inaccessible'). Two of the horses of Hades, Greek God of the Underworld. (See also NONIOS)

ABRAXAS: One of the horses of Eos, the Greek Dawn Goddess. (See also PHAETON)

AETHON, AETHIOPS, AMATHEA, ASTROPE, BRONTE, CHRONOS, EOUS, LAMPON, PHAETON, and PHLAEGON: The horses of Helios, the Greek Sun God. All winged, of dazzling white, and breathing fire, they drew his golden chariot, emerging at dawn from a swamp in Ethiopia and vanishing at sunset into the western ocean at the Hesperides. (Phaeton was also the name of Helios's son.) According to Eumelus of Corinth, Aethon turned the sky to make day and night, and Aethiops was a flaming horse who parched the grain. These two he named as male, while Bronte was a mare, responsible for thunder. Eumelus also named another mare as Sterops, producer of lightning.

ALIGERO CLAVILENO: ('Wooden-Pin Wing-Horse') The horse on which Don Quixote and Sancho Panza rode to the rescue of Dolorida and her companions. (See also DAPPLE, ROSINANTE)

ALSVIDUR, ARRAK: In Norse mythology, the two horses who drew the sun across the sky – though they were sometimes also attributed to the moon.

AMATHEA: ('Not Lingering') – see AETHON.

ARION: ('Warlike') Herakles's horse, given to him by Adrastos. It had been brought to Earth by the Greek Sea God Poseidon striking it with his trident. It had a human voice, and its right feet were like a man's.

ARRAK: (See ALSVIDUR).

ARVAKUR: ('Splendid') One of the horses of the Norse Sun God.

ASTROPE (See AETHON)

BALIOS: ('Swift') One of the horses given by the Greek Sea God Poseidon to Peleus, and later acquired by Achilles. Its sire was Zephyros, the West Wind, and its dam the harpy Swift-Foot. (See also XANTHOS)

BABIECA: ('Booby') The mount of the Spanish hero El Cid. He survived his master by two and a half years, but no one else was allowed to ride him. He was buried outside a monastery at Valencia, with two elm trees planted to mark the spot.

BAYARD: (Overlaps with BAJARDO) The black horse of the four sons of Aymon, which grew larger or smaller to match whichever of them mounted it. Tradition says its hoof-prints may still be seen near a village called Pay-Bayard (near

Belgium's most important megalithic site, Weris), and on a rock near Dinant. In the Ardennes, falling autumn leaves are said to be Bayard shedding his mane, and the hills are Bayard's back. The four sons of Aymon are said to represent the cardinal points. Although the Bayard stories have been attached to the period of Charlemagne (see BAJARDO below), a Belgian friend who knows the Ardennes well assures us that their essence is of pagan origin, from long before the time when Charlemagne Christianized the region. The name crept into English slang – up to the early eighteenth century, 'Bayard of ten toes' meant human feet, and 'ride Bayard's toes' meant to walk.

BAJARDO: (Overlaps with BAYARD, but said to be bright bay-coloured.) From the legend of Roland, nephew of Charlemagne. Roland is the hero of several French romances, and under the name Orlando, of the Italian romances *Orlando Furioso* and *Orlando Innamorato*, and of Shakespeare's *As You Like It*. Bajardo was the horse of Rinaldo, once owned by Amadia of Gaul. Found by the magician Malagigi in a cave guarded by a dragon, which he had to kill to reach it. Said to be still alive, but too swift a runner ever to be caught. (See also BRIGLIADORO, FRONTALETTO, RABICANO, VEGLIANTINO)

BENIK, ENIK, MENIK, SENIK: In Armenian mythology, these are the four horses who drew the Sun God's chariot.

BLACK BESS: The famous mare of the highwayman Dick Turpin. From his headquarters at the Swan Inn, at Woughton on the Green in Buckinghamshire, he is said once to have escaped pursuers by shoeing her backwards to confuse them. Turpin and Bess are both believed to haunt the district, as well as other places in England. (Prince Charles Edward, the Young Pretender, is said to have persuaded a blacksmith to use the same backwards-shoeing trick to avoid his pursuers in Mountcharles, County Donegal.)

BLACK MORO: The horse of the Welsh hero Elidir Mwynfawr, which could carry seven and a half people on its back.

BLACK OF SANGLIU, THE: One of two foals born at the same

time as the Irish hero Cuchulain, son of Deichtine and the god Lugh. they were both presented to the child and grew up with him. (See also THE GREY OF MACHA)

BLODIGHOFI: In Norse mythology, one of the horses of the Aesir.

BORAK, AL BORAK: ('Lightning') The horse sent by Gabriel to carry the Prophet Mohammed from Earth to the Seventh Heaven. Descriptions of it vary from it having the face and voice of a man and the wings of an eagle to being incredibly handsome but purely equine. It was finally taken back to Paradise.

BRIGLIADORE: ('Golden-Bridle') Sir Guyon's horse in Spenser's *Faery Queen*.

BRIGLIADORO: (Also 'Golden-Bridle') Orlando's horse in *Orlando Furioso*. Second only to BAJARDO (q.v.) in swiftness and ability. (See also FRONTALETTO, RABICANO, VEGLIANTINO)

BRONTE: (See AETHON)

BUCEPHALOS: ('Ox-Head') The mount of Alexander the Great, given to him by his father Philip of Macedon. Only Alexander could ride him, and he always knelt for his master to mount him. He was thirty years old when he died, and Alexander built a city called Bucephala to house his tomb.

BUCHESLOM: Horse of the Welsh hero Gwgawn of the Red Sword, mentioned in the Triads of Britain.

BUCKLAND SHAG, THE: A water-horse said to have murdered people at Buckland in Surrey.

CELER: (Swift') The horse of the Roman emperor Verus. It was fed on almonds and raisins, stalled in Verus's palace, and clothed in the imperial purple.

CHIRON: The most famous of the centaurs in Greek legend.

CHRONOS: (See AETHON)

CLEVER HANS: (KLUGE HANS) One of the ELBERFELD HORSES.

CLOVEN-HOOF: The horse of the Welsh hero Owain (son of Urien) mentioned in the Triads of Britain.

COMANCHE: Only survivor of the massacre of General Custer's

force at the Battle of Little Big Horn in 1876 and the mount of Captain Myles W. Keogh. He was wounded seven times. He was sent to Fort Lincoln, Dakota, and became a national legend; no one was allowed to ride him, and he was allowed to wander free wherever he was quartered. He died in 1893, aged thirty.

COPENHAGEN: The Duke of Wellington's horse.

CRIMEAN BOB: Survived the Charge of the Light Brigade at Balaclava, lived to be thirty, and was buried with military honours.

CULLTOPPR: The horse of Heimdahl, guardian of the bridge between Earth and the Norse Heaven.

CYLLAROS: (After Cylla in Troas) One of the horses of Castor and Pollux. (See also HARPAGOS)

DAPPLE: The ass of Sancho Panza, Don Quixote's squire. (See also ALIGERO CLAVINENO, ROSINANTE)

DICK, DICKY TATTON, DOBBY HORSE, YOUNG BALL: The Hallowe'en dummy horse of Cheshire.

DINOS: ('Marvel') One of the horses of Diomedes, King of Aetolia, who took part in the Trojan War. (See also LAMPON)

ELBERFELD HORSES: A group of German horses at the turn of the century who apparently developed the power to make mathematical calculations. The outstanding ones were CLEVER HANS (KLUGE HANS), MUHAMED and ZARIF.

ENIK: (See BENIK)

EOUS: (See AETHON)

ETASA: In Hindu mythology, the horse who draws the Sun across the sky.

ETHON: ('Fiery') One of the horses of Hector in the Trojan War. (See also GALATHE, PODARGE)

FALHOFNIR: In Norse mythology, one of the horses of the Aesir.

FIDDLE-BACK: Oliver Goldsmith's unfortunate pony.

FRONTALETTO: ('Little Head') Sacripant's horse in *Orlando Furioso*. (See also BAJARDO, BRIGLIADORO, RABICANO, VEGLIANTINO)

GALATHE: ('Cream-Coloured') One of Hector's horses. (See also ETHON, PODARGE)

GARDROFA: The dam of HOFVARPNIR.

GATO and MANTA: The two horses with which Professor A.F. Tschiffely made his 'impossible' overland journey in 1933 from Buenos Aires to Washington.

GILS, GLADR, GLAER: In Norse mythology, three of the horses of the Aesir.

GRANE: ('Grey') The marvellously swift horse of Siegfried, hero of German legend and Wagner's opera.

GREY OF MACHA, THE: One of two foals born at the same time as the Irish hero Cuchulain, son of Deichtine and the god Lugh. They were both presented to the child and grew up with him. Macha was a war goddess with equine associations. (See also THE BLACK OF SANGLIU)

GYLLIR: In Norse mythology, one of the horses of the Aesir.

HAIZUM: The horse of the Archangel Gabriel, named in the Koran.

HAMSKERPIR: Sire of HOFVARPNIR.

HARPAGOS: ('One that Carries Off Rapidly') One of the horses of Castor and Pollux. (See also CYLLAROS)

HIPPOCAMPES ('Coiling Horse') One of the horses of the Greek Sea God Poseidon. Its hindquarters were the tail of a fish or dragon.

HOFVARPNIR: The horse of Gna, messenger of the Norse Gods.

HRIMFAXI: In Norse mythology, the horse of the giantess Nott (Night), from whose bit fall the dewdrops found on the Earth in the morning.

INCITATUS: ('Spurred-On') The horse of the Roman emperor Caligula, whom he made a priest and a consul. Its stall was of marble, it drank wine out of a golden pail, had a retinue of slaves, and was host at many Imperial parties. The guests were expected to invite it in return.

KALKI: The white horse which will be the form Vishnu takes, or the mount he rides, in his final incarnation, according to Hindu mythology.

KHORS: Slavonic God of health and hunting, envisaged as a stallion.

KLUGE HANS: (CLEVER HANS) – one of the ELBERFELD HORSES.

LADY: The telepathic and sum-working filly owned by Mrs Claudia Fonda of Richmond, Virginia, in the 1920s.

LAMPON, LAMPOS: ('Bright One') One of the horses of Diomedes, king of Aetolia. (See also DINOS) Also named as one of the horses of the Sun God Helios (see AETHON).

LETTFETI: In Norse mythology, one of the horses of the Aesir.

LLUAGOR: ('Host-Splitter') The horse of the Welsh hero Caradawg Strong-Arm, mentioned in the Triads of Britain.

LONG-TONGUE: The horse of the Welsh hero Cadwallawn son of Cadfan, mentioned in the Triads of Britain.

MANTA: (See GATO)

MARENGO: Napoleon's horse.

MARI LLWYD: ('Grey Mare') A legendary Welsh horse whose wooden head is carried in procession round Carmarthen and Glamorgan villages at Christmas and the New Year, with traditional rituals. Said to have been a mare who had to be turned out of the Bethlehem stable to make room for the Holy Family, and who has been seeking shelter ever since.

MEG: Tam O'Shanter's mare in Robert Burns' poem of that name, who lost her tail to the young witch Cutty Sark ('short shirt or shift'). The tea-clipper *Cutty Sark*, preserved at Greenwich, has the witch as a figurehead and at sea, she always carried a horse's tail in her hand.

MEINLAS: ('Slender Grey') The horse of the Welsh hero Caswallawn son of Beli, mentioned in the Triads of Britain.

MELYNGAN MANGRE: ('Pale-Yellow-of-the-Stud') The horse of the Welsh god Lleu Llaw Gyffes, mentioned in the Triads of Britain.

MENIK: (See BENIK)

MUHAMED: One of the ELBERFELD HORSES.

NONIOS: One of the horses of the Greek Underworld God Hades. (See also ABASTER and ABATOS.)

OBRICK'S COLT: A colt said to haunt Cuthery Holt in Shropshire.

OLD ROWLEY: Charles II's horse.

PASSE-BREWELL: Sir Tristram's charger, named in Malory's *Morte D'Arthur*. When nobody could find the wandering Tristram, Dame Brangwayne, nurse to his lover Iseult, sought him 'long and widely'. When she did find him, she could not recognize the man she had known, but was able to identify him when she saw Passe-Brewell.

PEGASOS: ('Born Near the Source of the Ocean') The winged horse of Apollo and the Muses. Offspring of the Greek Sea God Poseidon and the Gorgon Medusa. Usually spelt Pegasus in English.

PHAETON: ('Shining One') One of the horses of Eos, the Greek Dawn Goddess. (See also ABRAXAS) Also named as one of the horses of the Sun God Helios (see AETHON) It was also the name of Helios's son.

PHALLAS: ('Stallion') The horse of Heraklios.

PHLAEGON: (see AETHON)

PODARGE: ('Swift-Foot') One of the horses of Hector in the Trojan War. Dam of XANTHOS. (See also ETHON, GALARTHE)

PYROEIS: (See AETHON)

RABICANO or RABICAN: ('Short-Tailed') Argalia's horse in *Orlando Innamorato*, and Astolpho's in *Orlando Furioso*. Its sire was wind, and its dam fire. It fed on unearthly food. (See also BAJARDO, BRIGLIADORO, FRONTALETTO, VEGLIANTINO)

RAKUSH: The mare of Rustum, the Persian Hercules; together they had to perform Seven Labours, including fighting with demons, a lion, a dragon, and a sorceress.

RONALD: The Earl of Cardigan's horse in the Charge of the Light Brigade at Balaclava.

ROSINANTE: ('Formerly a Hack') Don Quixote's horse, all skin and bone. (See also ALIGERO CLAVILENO, DAPPLE)

SENIK: (See BENIK)

SHINING MANE: The white steed of Dag, the Norse god of the day. It spread its light over the whole world.

SILFRINTOPPR, SKEIDBRIMIR, SKINFAXI: In Norse mythoogy, three of the horses of the Aesir.

SLEIPNIR: Odin's grey horse, which had eight legs, and could traverse land or water or travel through the air. It symbolized the wind which can blow over land and sea from the eight principal points. After the death of Balder, it was lent to the blind Hermod, who had been tricked by Loki into accidentally killing Balder. Hermod rode it to the underworld to plead with the Goddess Hela for his restoration to life. Hela would have released Balder if everyone would weep for him; only the giantess Thaukt refused, so he remained dead.

SPLENDID MANE: The horse of the Irish and Manx sea god Mannanán mac Lir.

STEROPS: (See AETHON)

SURREY: The horse of King Richard III, killed at the Battle of Bosworth, leaving the doomed king to fight on foot. He is named in Shakespeare's play ('Saddle white Surrey for the field tomorrow') and his loss is immortalized by Richard's cry: 'A horse! a horse! my kingdom for a horse!'

SVADILFARI, SYNIR: In Norse mythology, two of the horses of the Aesir.

TANGIE: A demon sea-horse said to have terrorized the area of Fitful Head, Mainland, Shetland, pursuing girls on the shore in search of a human bride. He used to be ridden by a sub-human sheep-stealer called Black Eric, who was fought and finally thrown to death off the Head by a courageous crofter called Sandy Breamer, in spite of Tangie's efforts to protect him.

VEGLIANTINO: ('Little Vigilant One') Orlando's steed. Called in French VEILLANTIF and in France Orlando is Roland. (See also BAJARDO, BRIGLIADORO, FRONTALETTO, RABICANO)

WEEPING ROGER: The horse which started Henry Blake, of the Llanybyther Horse Centre in Carmarthenshire, on his researches into horse telepathy.

XANTHOS: ('Chestnut-Coloured') One of the horses of Achilles. When Achilles unjustly rebuked him, he announced the hero's approaching death. His sire was Zephyros, the West Wind, and his dam PODARGE (q.v.)

YOUNG BALL: (See DICK)

ZARIF: One of the ELBERFELD HORSES.

Bibliography

Apuleius, Lucius – *The Golden Ass* (Robert Graves trans., Penguin, London, 1950)

Barber, Richard and Riches, Anne – *A Dictionary of Fabulous Beasts* (Macmillan, London, 1971)

Bardens, Dennis – *Psychic Animals* (Robert Hale Ltd., London, 1987)

Bede, The Venerable – *The Ecclesiastical History of the English Nation* (c. 700 AD; J.M Dent, London, 1910)

Binder, Pearl – *Magic Symbols of the World* (Hamlyn, London, 1972)

Bonwick, James – *Irish Druids and Old Irish Religions* (first published 1894; Dorset Press, USA, 1986)

Bord, Janet & Colin – *The Secret Country* (Paul Elek Ltd., London, 1976). *Earth Rites: Fertility Practices in Pre–Industrial Britain* (Granada, London, 1982) *Mysterious Britain* (Garnstone Press, London, 1972)

Boutell, Charles – *The Handbook to English Heraldry* (Reeves & Turner, London, 1914)

Brewer, Rev. E. Cobham – *Dictionary of Phrase and Fable* (14th edn., Cassell, London, 1989)

Budge, E.A. Wallis – *Amulets and Talismans* (Collier Books, Macmillan, New York, 1970. Originally published 1930 as *Amulets and Superstitions*)

Burton, Maurice – *The Sixth Sense of Animals* (J.M. Dent & Sons, London, 1973)

Campbell, Joseph – *The Masks of God: Primitive Mythology* (Viking Press, New York, 1959; Souvenir Press, London, 1973)

Cavendish, Richard – *The Black Arts* (Routledge & Kegan Paul, London, 1967)

Chetwynd, Tom – *A Dictionary of Symbols* (Granada Publishing, St Albans, Herts, 1982)

Clébert, Jean-Paul – *The Gypsies* (English translation by Charles Duff, Vista Books, London, 1963)
Coolidge, Dane & Mary Roberts – *The Navaho Indians* (Houghton Mifflin, Boston, 1930)
Davies, Hunter – *Book of British Lists* (Hamlyn Paperbacks, London, 1980)
Davis, R.H.C. – *The Normans and Their Myth* (Thames & Hudson, London, 1976)
Deane, Tony & Shaw, Tony – *The Folklore of Cornwall* (B.T. Batsford, London, 1975)
Delsol, Paula – *Chinese Horoscopes* (Mercure de France, 1969; English trans. Pictorial Presentations Ltd., London, 1973, and paperback Pan Books, London, 1973)
Deren, Maya – *Divine Horsemen* (Thames & Hudson, London, 1953. Paperback version titled *The Voodoo Gods*, Paladin, St Albans, Herts. 1975)
Durdin–Robertson, Lawrence – *Goddesses of Chaldaea, Syria and Egypt* (Cesara Publications, Enniscorthy, Ireland, 1975). *Goddesses of India, Tibet, China and Japan* (Cesara, 1976). *Juno Covella: Perpetual Calendar of the Fellowship of Isis* (Cesara, 1982)
Fabricius, Johannes – *Alchemy: The Mediaeval Alchemists and their Royal Art* (Rosenkilde & Bagger, Copenhagen, 1976; revised edn. Aquarian Press, Wellingborough, Northants, 1989)
Farmer, David Hugh – *The Oxford Dictionary of Saints* (Oxford University Press, Oxford, 1978)
Farrar, Janet & Stewart – *Eight Sabbats for Witches* (Robert Hale Ltd., London, 1981) *The Witches' Way* (Hale, 1984) *The Witches' Goddess* (Hale, 1987) *The Life and Times of a Modern Witch* (Headline Books, London, 1987) *The Witches' God* (Hale, 1989) *Spells and How They Work* (Hale, 1990) (All also Phoenix Publishing, Custer, WA, USA)
Fire, John/Lame Deer and Richard Erdoes – *Lame Deer, Sioux Medicine Man* (Davis–Poynter Ltd., London, 1973. Quartet Books paperback, London, 1980)
Folklore, Myths and Legends of Britain (23 authors) (Reader's Digest Association, London, 1973)
Frazer, Sir James G. – *The Golden Bough* (abridged edition, Macmillan, London, paperback 1974; our page references are to this reprint, more easily obtained than the 1922 original).
Friend, J.N. – *Demonology, Sympathetic Magic and Witchcraft*

(Charles Griffin, London, 1961)
Genius of China, The (Several authors, foreword by Lord Trevelyan. Times Newspapers Ltd., London, 1973)
Graves, Robert – *The White Goddess* (3rd edition, Faber & Faber, London, 1952)
Green, Andrew – *Our Haunted Kingdom* (Wolfe Publishing, London, 1973)
Gregory, Lady – *Visions and Beliefs in the West of Ireland* (Colin Smythe Ltd., Gerrards Cross, Bucks., 1970. First published 1920)
Guiley, Rosemary Ellen – *The Encyclopedia of Witches and Witchcraft* (Facts on File Publications, New York and Oxford, 1989)
Herm, Gerhard – *The Celts* (English translation, Weidenfeld & Nicolson, London, 1976)
Hill, Ruth Beebe – *Hanta Yo: An American Saga* (Doubleday, New York, 1979)
Hole, Christina – *British Folk Customs* (Hutchinson, London, 1976) *Witchcraft in England* (Fitzhouse Books, London, 1977)
Holy Bible, The – Quotations are from the Authorized (King James) version except where otherwise indicated.
Hope, Murry – *Practical Celtic Magic* (The Aquarian Press, Wellingborough, Northants., 1987)
Hughes, Pennethorne – *Witchcraft* (Longmans, Green, London, 1952; paperback Penguin, Harmondsworth, Middlesex, 1965)
Jung, Carl Gustav – *The Collected Works of C.G. Jung*, 2nd Edition, Vol.12: *Psychology and Alchemy* (Routledge & Kegan Paul, London, 1968)
Kramer, Heinrich & Sprenger, James – *Malleus Maleficarum* (trans. by Montague Summers, Arrow Books, London, 1971)
Larousse Encyclopaedia of Mythology (Hamlyn, London, 1959)
Leek, Sybil – *Diary of a Witch* (Prentice-Hall, New Jersey, 1969; paperback New American Library, New Jersey, 1969)
Lethbridge, T.C. – *Witches: Investigating an Ancient Religion* (Routledge & Kegan Paul, London, 1962)
Lissner, Ivar – *The Living Past* (English trans. J. Maxwell Brownjohn, Jonathan Cape, London, 1957)
Logan, Patrick, M.D. – *Making the Cure: A Look at Irish Folk Medicine* (Talbot Press, Dublin, 1972)
MacCana, Proinsias – *Celtic Mythology* (Hamlyn, London, 1970)
McCone, Kim – *Pagan Past and Christian Present* (An Sagat, Maynooth, 1990)

McEwan, Graham J. – *Mystery Animals of Britain and Ireland* (Robert Hale Ltd., London, 1986)
Mac Manus, Dermot – *The Middle Kingdom: The Faerie World of Ireland* (Colin Smythe, Gerrards Cross, Bucks, 1973)
MacNeill, Máire – *The Festival of Lughnasa* (Oxford University Press, London, 1962; 2 vols. paperback, Comhairle Bhealoideas Eireann, University College Dublin, 1982)
Markale, Jean – *Women of the Celts* (English translation) (Gordon Cremonesi, London, 1972; Inner Traditions International, Rochester, Vermont)
Mathers, Powys (trans.) – *The Book of the Thousand Nights and One Night* (Folio Society, London, 1959)
Mawer, Allen – *The Vikings* (Cambridge University Press, 1930)
Muir, Frank and Jamie – *A Treasury of Christmas* (Robson Books, London, 1981)
Naddair, Kaledon – *Keltic Folk and Faerie Tales* (Century Hutchinson Ltd., London, 1987)
Newman, Paul – *Gods and Graven Images: The Chalk Hill-Figures of Britain* (Robert Hale, London, 1987)
O'Sullivan, Sean – *Legends from Ireland* (B.T. Batsford, London, 1977)
de Paor, Maire and Liam – *Early Christian Ireland* (Thames and Hudson, London, 1958)
Partridge, Eric – *A Dictionary of Historical Slang* (Penguin Books, Harmondsworth, Middlesex, 1972)
Phillips, Guy Ragland – *Brigantia: A Mysteriography* (Routledge & Kegan Paul, London, 1976)
Pinsent, John – *Greek Mythology* (Hamlyn, London, 1969)
Power, Patrick C. – *The Book of Irish Curses* (Mercier Press, Cork, 1974)
Predicting the Future (various authors) (Tiger Books International, London, 1990)
Radford, E. & M.A. – *Encyclopaedia of Superstition* (Hutchinson, London, 1948)
Ross, Anne – *Pagan Celtic Britain* (Routledge & Kegan Paul, London 1967) *Everyday Life of the Pagan Celts* (B.T. Batsford, Ltd., London, 1970)
Rothenberg, Jerome (editor) – *Technicians of the Sacred: A Range of Poetries from Africa, America, Asia & Oceania* (Doubleday & Co., Inc., New York, 1968)
St Clair, David – *Drum and Candle: First-hand Experiences and Accounts of Voodoo and Spiritism* (Macdonald, London, 1971)
Spence, Lewis – *The Mysteries of Britain* (Aquarian Press,

London, 1928)
Starkey, Dinah – *Mermaids, Moonrakers and Hobgoblins* (Kaye & Ward, London, 1977)
Sykes, Egerton – *Everyman's Dictionary of Non–Classical Mythology* (J.M. Dent, London, revised, 1968)
Taylor, Lord William – *The Mycenaeans* (Thames & Hudson, London, 1965)
Toynbee, Arnold – *Mankind and Mother Earth* (Oxford University Press, Oxford, 1976)
Waddell, Helen (trans.) – *Beasts and Saints* (Constable, London, 1934)
Waite, Arthur Edward – *The Pictorial Key to the Tarot* (with new material, University Books Inc., New York, 1960; originally published 1910)
Wallechinsky, David, Wallace, Irving & Wallace, Amy – *The Book of Lists* (Corgi Books, London, 1978)
Wilcock, John – *A Guide to Occult Britain* (Sidgwick & Jackson, London, 1976)
Wilhelm, Richard – *I Ching* or *Book of Changes* (English trans. by Cary F. Baynes, 3rd edn., Routledge & Kegan Paul, London, 1968)

Index